Daily Obama Jokes
Saves The Country

By
James Buffington

ISBN 1448669812
EAN-13 9781448669813.

Introduction

The battle is on for United States. Socialists have hijacked the Democratic party and are striving to bring all under their odorous control.

One voice stands firm, showing them to be the misguided masters wannabee that they are. The blog dailyobamajokes.com mixes with with the rapier of reason to light our way through this dark night political emptiness.

Here now are the first 90 days worth of entries to bring light to the landscape political.

Daily Obama Jokes 04/06/09

How many Obamas does it take to change a light bulb?
None! That's a union job!

What is Obama's favorite movie?
"Clueless"

Comment:

Remember when vetoless George was spending money like a drunken sailor? The Dems challenged all that spending, demanding to know how the increasing deficits would be paid for. The Republican answer, met with derision by the Dems, was that we would grow the economy and grow our way out of the deficit.

Last week former Clinton labor sec Robert Reich was on cnbc. With the deficits mounting to 26 per cent of gdp he was asked how the Dems plan to pay for it. His answer? To grow the economy. Same one the Republicans gave that Reich and the Dems scoffed at.

Truth, it seems, has become a matter of convenience.

Daily Obama Jokes 04/07/09

There once was a Prez named Obama

Whose socialist ways caused a trauma

Our taxes shot higher

Our lives, they grew dire

And all as he laughed, "Yo' mama!"

How did Obama get that great smile?

Eating bananas sideways.

Liberal Misdirection:

I've been annoyed for years by the liberal media
trying to associate fascism with the conservatives,
We repeatedly see pictures from Nazi Germany tied
to politicos like George Bush and commentators
like Glenn Beck. Either liberals don't understand
what Nazis stood for, or they don't want you to.

Nazi stands for National Socialist. This was a subset
of fascism and a left wing political movement.
Hitler incorporated German nationalism and his
personal hatred of Jews into the mix. These two
elements are Hitler specifics, nor rightly part of
fascism per se.

Hitler came to power as the Depression gripped Germany. He fed on the people's fear. He gave great speeches. He engineered a strong economic recovery and nationalized the banks before moving to other segments of the economy. He was very popular.

Any of this sound familiar?

Obama jokes 04/08/09

Why does Obama spend 11 am to 11:15 by himself in the oval office every morning?

He's in time out.

Why do so few people laugh at Obama jokes?

Liberals don't think they're funny. Conservatives don't think they're jokes.

Nazis Continued.

I became aware of how powerful the liberal media's tie in of Nazism to conservatives had become a few years back. My wife, a college grad, well paid professional with a Mensa level i.q., and I were watching an old Game Show Network program called Inquizition. The question to the contestants was simple: Is Nazism a left wing or right wing movement? My wife blurted out "right wing!" I told her no, it was left wing. She gave me a look that was a cross between incredulity and pity mixed with a healthy dose of surprise. As I recall all three contestants answered right wing. All were shocked when the host answered left wing.

To me this shows just how powerfully the liberal media can sell and promote an untruth. One of the greatest services that could be performed for the voters of this country would be to get the message out that Nazis are left wing.

Nazi

It's not National Conservative

It's not National Republican

IT'S NATIONAL SOCIALISM!

Daily Obama Jokes 04/09/09

Obama's speeches are loud, full of hot air and make you feel good.

Sort of like passing gas.

Conservatives curb their dogs

Democrats curb other people's dogs.

A Final Note On Nazis

The Democratic party has been, frankly, hijacked by socialists. They couldn't get anywhere with their own party, so took over a branded one. The far left, powered by organizations like moveon.org, have been funded by George Soros, an alleged, at least, Nazi sympathizer in WW2 Hungary. Militant left wing organizations join in attacking Jews and Israel, physically attack speakers who disagree with them, attempt to silence those who oppose them, and try to intimidate Democratic politicians who won't play ball. Remember Joe Lieberman?

George Soros recently announced the world needs a new world currency, replacing the dollar as the reserve currency. That would trash the value of the dollar. Soros plays in those markets. I wonder if he has a bet down? And on what side of the table?

Are you a long time democrat? Is this the party you joined those many years ago? I think you've been hijacked.

And, yes, I fear it could happen here.

Daily Obama Jokes 04/10/09

Why is Michelle upset with Queen Pelosi?

Pelosi thinks Barack has just the right sized stimulus package.

Why will Obama win in 2012

Once you've gone Barack, you never go back.

Oh, Arrggh!

An Obama science advisor has advised we adopt radical means to fight "global warming." His idea is to shoot light reflecting substances into the atmosphere to deflect sunlight and cool the planet.

Sigh.

News flash! In the past the planet has been a complete snowball. In the past the planet has been a pole to pole swamp. It heats up. It cools down. Through natural processes. These guys seem to think that the Earth should never change. They look around and say "It should always be like this. Change is bad."

Change is natural. Normal. An integral part of evolution.

I wonder what these guys would say if our civilization arose, say, in 1399 a.d. The Earth went through a "mini ice age" from 1,000 to 1,400. It was significantly colder than it is today. What would they have screamed then? "Stop building campfires! Put out that torch!"

And exactly how would they know the difference between a "man made" and natural shift in climate trends anyways?

Seems to me the greenies are fueled by arrogance, a desire for control and kids who want to play with matches.

Daily Obama Jokes 04/11/09

What did Obama and Indian president Patil discuss when they met?

They told Sikh jokes.

What is Queen Pelosi's favorite recipe?

A recipe for disaster.

One thing I hate about greenies is the chain yanking.

Let's take polar bears.

We get treated to cute looking polar bears struggling on ice floes. We're told global warming is killing them off. We must return to the Stone Age or they will all die. Sniff.

The fact is there are 25,000 polar bears in North America. Around 1970 there were 5,000. Sounds like a nice comeback. Those cute polar bears are, by the way, mean spirited beasts that would rip your head off in a New York minute.

We see the bears on an ice floe. How many bears got trapped on ice floes in 1980? 1940? 1900? Ice has always broken off the arctic and I'm reasonably confident bears have been getting trapped on them as long as they've existed. These icebergs can be quite large and dangerous. Remember the Titanic?

I've no doubt bears being trapped on big bergs is nothing new.

Polar bears endangered at 25,000? How many were there in 1900? 1800? 1500? What is the right number of bears? The greenies never tell us. As if they knew. 25,000, for all I know, is the right number for the habitat.

It's not about the polar bears. It's about controlling you and your life.

There are only about 400 California condors, up from a low of about 20. If it were really about preventing the extinction of a species then why aren't we being inundated with condor commercials? Videos of cute little carrion eaters bursting forth from their eggs? The lone bird ripping the entrails out of a hapless rodent?

Because it's not about conservation. Just good, old chain yanking control.

Sunday, April 12, 2009

Daily Obama Jokes 04/12/09

Easter Sunday

He Is Risen

Yes, Obama got up at seven thirty this morning, went potty, had breakfast.....

Seriously, Happy Easter!

Daily Obama Jokes 04/13/09

How does Obama now define "enemy combatant?"

"Republican."

Obama was touring the farm belt, looking to sell some more giveaways. At one farm flies kept buzzing around his head, annoying him greatly.

"What kind of flies are these?" asked Obama of the farmer.

"Those are horse flies," answered the farmer. "You usually find them around a horse's ass."

"Are you implying I'm a horse's ass?"

"No sir, but those flies are hard to fool."

Amazingly, greenies can change direction at a moment's notice, even if it's to stop ideas they presented. Wind power is a good example. They sold this for years. Now that it may start adding to our power supply it must be stopped! Birds fly into the arms of the wind turbines. And wind turbines have to be constructed far from the power grid. This means new transmission lines would have to be built. Can't have any nasty old power towers build in the grasslands, forest, desert, etc.

Give me a break!

They also ignore any innovations that would disempower their attempts at controlling the rest of society. MIT has, for example, developed a methodology for atmospheric scrubbers. Each would remove 18 tons of carbon dioxide per year from the air. Ever hear one word about that from the greenies? Nope. Can't advance their control freak plans to drive our society back into a more primitive state,

Ever hear of Project Iter? Didn't think so. This is a prototype fusion power plant being built in France (France! Why not Texas or Montana?) and scheduled for completion around 2016. Forget conventional nuclear plants, coal fired plants, solar and wind. Perfect fusion and that is the way to go.

But you never hear the greenies talk about this. Promoting a positive idea would end their ability to complain and try and control how the rest of us do things.

Lastly, you hear no talk of hybrid reactors. The main problems with conventional reactors are 1. they leave significant waste that is very hazardous and needs to be stored and 2. like oil, uranium is a dwindling resource. No one is making more. A hybrid reactor combines fission and fusion principles and burns up as fuel 99% of the toxic waste. The University of Texas at Austin has plans for one. So why aren't the greenies and media talking this up?

The answer, as always, is that it's not about the environment, it's about control.

Why is Obama such a party animal?

He loves to socialize

Why did Obama bow to the Saudi king?

The teleprompter was on the floor.

Taxes: where we got screwed.

Initially our forefathers did not give the government the power to tax income. They did not foresee what was to come and thus built insufficient safeguards for personal property into the document.

Later the progressives, our first liberals, got through an amendment allowing the feds to tax income. It had no limitations on what the government could do. No safeguards for the people. The initial tax was supposed to target just a few people and at a miniscule rate.

It was the camel sticking it's head in the tent.

With infinite taxing power now at it's disposal, congress soon was raising rates and lowering thresholds. Eventually tax rates hit ninety percent at the upper brackets and all but the lowest strata paid something.

Now the tax code is being used as a social weapon. About half the country pays no taxes.

Others pay an unfair burden as people get to vote themselves other people's money.

And congress revels in and abuses a power it was never intended to have and which it usurped through a legal fiat.

If you wonder what it is you smell this time of year, it's the rest of the camel invading your tent.

Daily Obama Jokes 04/15/09

How many union workers does it take to change a light bulb?

"What's it to ya?"

What advice did Bill Clinton give Obama on foreign relations?

"Don't have any."

Every year we hear the litany of phrases. Tax Reform. Tax Simplification. Tax Reduction.

 Blah, blah, blah.

It hasn't happened and it won't.

Our poor handling of the Constitution in this regard has given almost unlimited power to congress. The tax code can be used to punish those who don't play ball and reward those who do. States, industries, and sociocultural groups all feel the touch of the velvet fisted glove.

Further, it has given rise to the entire lobbying industry. As lobbyists curry favor amongst the powerful our congressional leaders receive perks, ego strokes and a feeding of their sense of importance and power. Worship at the altar of the tax break.

You get hours of forms to fill. An expensive tax preparer to pay. Convoluted "tax savings" plans like IRAs, 401Ks, and Flexible Spending Accounts. These things sound good on the surface, but would be unnecessary with a proper tax code. They really create jobs for paper shufflers and administrators while feeding you the illusion that the government is generously allowing you to keep more of your money.

Worst of all tax policy and positions can be tailored to the garnering of votes. Nothing like promising your voters other people's money to assure popularity. "Hey, let's you and me get together and mug that guy. He can afford it."

As long as power, taxes and congress are tied together the last thing we can expect is any real change. Sorry, that's just the way it is.

Daily Obama Jokes 04/16/09

What is the first thing Obama did when he heard he won the election?

He was so happy he flapped his ears and flew around the room.

What should he have done?

Demand a recount.

A Tax Alternative.

Now that the pain we all feel for the sake of misappropriated congressional power Is over for another year let's, just for fun, look at some alternatives to income theft, er, taxes. Basic ideas to think about, of course, not full fledged proposals.

First up: A national property tax.

Consider. No forms to fill out ever. Value assessments are done locally. Collection methods are already in place. Just piggyback on those. The tax rate could be graduated, based on the value of the property so the poor pay little or nothing and the wealthy pay more.

No convoluted set of deductions, no tax preparers to pay, hours of your life back from preparing forms and saving and sorting receipts, no class warfare, no irs, no audits. Paper pushing administrative jobs that build costs into our economy, like IRAs, 401Ks and Flexible Spending Accounts would no longer have a purpose.

Everyone knows in advance what will be due.

An estimated 14 trillion dollars is hiding from the tax man overseas. No reason for that anymore and who would care anyways?

Commercial properties would be taxed at their full value. No federal tax breaks due to local abatements.

Lobbying for tax breaks ends.

I can't imagine a better platform to build a tax system on.

Daily Obama Jokes 04/17/09

With Obama in charge of energy policy what natural resource will he exploit?

The taxpayer.

Obama's economic policy has me back on my feet. Last week they repo'd my car.

A True Sin Tax

Everybody loves a sin tax. They give one a moral justification to vote themselves other people's money. "Oh. Look. They smoke cigarettes! That's morally wrong! Let's beat them up and mug them and take their money!"

Why not have a real Sin Tax?

Let's add on a 50% federal penalty to every criminal and civil fine in the country. You get a $100 speeding ticket, you pay $150.

A corporation gets a $100,000 fine for something, they pay $150,000.

The calculation would be automatic, the courts are already there to handle collection, and people who have actually broken laws and/or rules get to pay.

Sounds like a plan to me. Got a light?

Daily Obama Jokes 04/18/09

There once was a millionaire who had a live in butler. Every Monday the butler had the night off and attended a meeting of the socialist party. Then one Monday night the butler stayed home and read a book in his room. The millionaire was curious, but said nothing.

The following Monday the butler again stayed home. The next morning the millionaire asked his butler, "How come you've stayed home the last two Mondays? You always looked forward to your socialist party meetings."

"The last time I went they announced the results of a study. If all the wealth of the United States were divided amongst the citizens everyone would have $10,000."

"So?"

"Well, sir, I have $20,000."

A Sort Of Sin Tax

Here's one last idea for an alternative tax before moving on to other topics.

Let's tax birth control!

A 10 cent per condom tax sounds like a winner to me. And perhaps a 1 dollar tax on a month's supply of birth control pills.

People aren't going to stop having sex over a little tax. It's a sure fire fundraiser. True, the

25

devout Catholics will get a break, but the rest of us won't be singing "I've Got Rhythm."

And they said it couldn't be taxed.

Just to be safe, though, if I were president I wouldn't present this idea until my second term....

Daily Obama Jokes 04/19/09

Biden and Obama were talking one day and Biden said, "You know, maybe we should listen to the Republicans more. They are smart businessmen."

"What do you mean?"

"Come with me and I'll show you."

So they left the White House and Joe took Obama to Harry's Hardware Emporium, run by Harry Mercer, a known Republican supporter. They entered and found Harry at the counter.

"Excuse me, " said Biden. "I need a set of left handed screwdrivers."

"One minute," replied Harry, and he disappeared into the back. He returned a minute later with a set of screwdrivers. "Here you go. One set of left handed screwdrivers. That'll be $29.95."

The politicians made their purchase and left.

"There, you see. Left handed screwdrivers! I told you they were smart!"

"What's so smart about that?" challenged Obama. "He just happened to have a set in the back!"

Wealth Reduction

Socialists believe wealth redistribution is the solution to social ills and poverty. In actually wealth redistribution leads to wealth destruction. Their belief is rooted in several simplistic fallacies.

The first of these is that wealth is a static measure. That the amount of wealth does not change. Just as there is so only so much oil, or coal, or uranium, they implicitly believe wealth is an absolute.

While it is true that at any instant there is so much wealth, that amount changes second by second. Wealth can be created or destroyed. Let's say all the wealth of the country was redistributed in the summer of 2007. The stock market was nearing its all time high. Everyone would have gotten more. The same result at the beginning of March 2009 would have had a far lesser result. The market was down over 50% and each would have received less. This wealth reduction was the result of market forces acting on the perceived value and earnings power of companies.

Since then, as earnings have started appearing better than expected, mark to market accounting rules been modified and some credit bottlenecks alleviated, the market has risen 25%.

The wealth here is not an intrinsic thing, it's a function of what people are willing to pay. When people are willing to pay more for what you have, you are wealthier. When they are willing to pay less you are less wealthy.

Now imagine how these companies would be valued if we redistributed them. We socialize Coca Cola. Every family in America gets, for the sake of argument, 3 shares. Demand for the shares would fall. There would be no efficient market for their exchange. The value of the shares would plummet.

Redistribution would destroy wealth. And while wealth can come back when it's concentrated and traded in reasonably efficient markets, there would be no mechanism of return from this diffusion.

Wealth wouldn't be redistributed, it would be destroyed.

Daily Obama Jokes 04/20/09

Why is Obama such a big supporter of public housing?

He lives in it. Why not everyone?

Michelle's birthday is always a problem for Obama. He likes to get her something practical and she always gets upset and cries.

So this year he's getting her handkerchiefs.

Wealth redistribution attacks the very mechanisms that create wealth and prosperity. In order to do good there must be concentrations of wealth. Divide everything up according to some philosophical view other than earned merit and movements forward grind to a halt. Who is there to build a building? How can one open a new restaurant or other business? How would funding become available for new research? And on and on.

For progress to occur wealth must exist in concentrations and must be given the opportunity to propagate itself.

Daily Obama Jokes 04/21/09

Now that the Obama girls have a dog Michelle is being very firm.

"Having a dog means learning responsibility. You will feed the dog twice a day. You will walk the dog three times a day. And you will clean up the dog's poop. Is that understood?"

"Yes, dear," replied Barack.

"Why were the Republicans disappointed in the Obama's choice of dogs?

They were hoping he'd get one named "Puddles."

The Roll Call

It's hard to believe that anyone could buy into a socialist agenda. One does not even have to discuss politics or philosophy. One just has to look at the roll call of history:

Lenin

Stalin

Hitler

Mussolini

Franco

Mao

Castro

Chavez

Which of these guys would you like to live under?

In point of fact all totalitarian states must move left. It becomes an imperative to control the people, to control the economy, to control business, to control speech, to ultimately try and control minds.

These are the methods of the socialist state.

There is not and never has been a conservative dictatorship. With an emphasis on personal freedom and responsibility, conservativism (which is not, by the way, the same thing as being a republican) is diametrically the opposite of socialism. Always has been. Always will be.

Daily Obama Jokes 04/22/09

What's black and white and red all over?

Transcriptions of Obama's speeches.

Obama is doing the job of three men.

Larry, Curly and Moe.

More On Money

I mentioned previously that money needs to be concentrated to do any good. It has one more property that needs to be discussed. It must flow freely, circulating through the body of the nation, to keep the muscles of the economy healthy.

Doesn't that contradict what I said about concentration of wealth? Not at all. There is a difference between wealth and money. The wealth of the rich comes in the form of assets. Their money is invested in bonds, stocks and business. It is used to finance and build. The wealthy circulate money by putting it to work in countless ways.

View each concentration as a heart. It beats, pumping the blood of money through the body. It flows, returning to the" heart", and gets pumped out again.

Socialism destroys this dynamic. It stifles the vibrancy, the growth, the innovation that is needed for a free society and economy. It reduces money to a mere mush used for sustenance and little else.

Daily Obama Jokes 04/23/09

John Kerry, briefcase in hand, entered a Boston pub, sauntered to the bar and ordered a Manhattan.

His drink arrived and he downed it quickly. "Hey," he exclaimed, "that was the best Manhattan I've ever had. I think I'll have another."

So the bartender brought over a second drink. Kerry quickly downed it, too.

'That one was even better!"

"Can I get you one more, sir?" asked the barkeep.

"No, two is my limit," replied Kerry as he put his money on the counter. "But let me reward you for drinks well made." With that Kerry opened his briefcase and plopped a live lobster on the counter. "This is for you."

"Hey, thanks!" beamed the bartender. "I'll have him for dinner."

"Oh, he's had dinner," said Kerry. "Why don't you take him to a movie?"

Danger, Will Robinson! Danger, Will Robinson!

Before beginning let me make very clear this entry is not about torture. It is about free speech. Where ever you stand on torture doesn't matter.

Recently there has been talk of prosecuting legal advisors to President Bush for the perspectives they gave on what constitutes torture. What they did was examine the law, definitions supplied by congress in 1995 and give an opinion. What they did was speak freely.

Prosecute someone for this and we are all in trouble. If professional lawyers can be prosecuted for giving an opinion to the government while employed by that same government to do exactly that, then where do the rest of us stand? Which opinions can we express that won't get us sent to jail? Is the only speech that's free that which agrees with the administration?

If you are for or against torture, you have a right to speak.

If you are for or against a war, you have a right to speak.

If you are for or against mom's apple pie, you have a right to speak.

Even considering prosecuting these guys for rendering an opinion threatens that right for all of us. I fear we have some very dangerous people in power. And I will say so.

Excuse me, there's a knock at my door....

Daily Obama Jokes 04/24/09

What did Michelle say when Obama first asked her to take his name?

She refused at first. She thought "Barack" would be a silly name for a girl.

How is Obama like Jesus?

He thinks we're fishes and takes our bread.

More On Torture.

Once again I'm not commenting pro or con. There are good arguments, depending on perspective, on each side. What does irk me, though, are arguments which are invalid. One such is that torture is ineffective.

To approach this I must be honest, brutally so, with myself. You can bandy about all the intellectualisms you want on either side. It doesn't matter. When I look myself in the eye I must admit that I would eventually spill the beans. I'm no hero, Not a bastion of macho. I'm just an ordinary person. And, faced with sufficient physical persuasion, I would talk.

I probably shouldn't make this kind of confession publicly, but it's true. That being said, the argument that torture is ineffective vanishes, No amount of spurious false intellectualism can overcome the reality of my self knowledge.

If you think torture is ineffective, ask yourself what you would do if you had a secret and the bad guys wired a car battery to your genitals. Honestly, would you talk in time? If so, then you have to admit that the argument is nothing but rhetorical tactical positioning. And if you wouldn't talk? You are either deluding yourself, or you're a better man than I, Gunga Din.

Daily Obama Jokes 04/25/09

An aide dashed into Secretary Clintons's
office. "There's been an earthquake in South
America! 6 Brazilians are dead."
"That's awful!" exclaimed Hillary. "But tell me,
how many are there in a brazillion?"

Obamamerica
"Take my liberty
And give me debt."

A last comment on torture (for now).

A second lie crops up in the torture debate.
Those against torture claim that you get bad
information, that people say anything to get you
to stop.
These people are either naïve or expect you to be.
In any interrogation, despite the methodology, a
mix of questions are asked. Some you know the
answers to, some you want to know the answers
to. The quality of information you get for the
questions you know the answer to forms a
baseline for judging the viability of the remaining
answers.
Properly done, information obtained by physical
persuasion can be quite reliable.

Let's move on to some more pleasant stuff....

Daily Obama Jokes 04/26/09

Daily Obama Jokes 04/26/09

When he ran for his first office Obama was unhappy with some things said about him in a local paper and threatened to sue. The paper denied any wrong doing. When a reporter asked if he planned on pressing his suit Obama replied, "Of course! I can't campaign in wrinkled clothes!"

How did Obama get a splinter in his finger? Scratching his head.

Congress Costs Jobs

Remember a while back when the heads of the auto companies appeared before congress? They had their heads handed to them for taking private jets to Washington. Splashed that all over the front pages and across the airwaves.
There's a second leg to this story that isn't getting the same attention.
Immediately after this occurred companies began canceling bookings on private flights and stopped making new ones. Orders for new jets by companies disappeared down a rabbit hole into Neverland..
The result?
Private service airlines and manufacturers have laid off over 60% of their personnel.
Congressional talk caused good paying jobs to walk.
People and companies with money stopped spending it.
Other people lost their jobs.
Those people are forced to cut back on their spending...
Affecting those who partially depend on that spending....
A pebble tossed in the water, expanding its wave.....

I think we need to reopen the purely political piece of trash rhetoric laughingly referred to as "trickle down."

Daily Obama Jokes 04/27/09
Daily Obama Jokes 04/27/09

Obama is the second best thing to ever come out of Chicago.
The first best? An empty bus.

Michelle can drink Barack under the table. After all, 1 gal holds 4 qts.

Pin Action Economics

I've mentioned previously that for an economy to be healthy and growing money must flow freely through the nation as blood through the body.
Jim Cramer refers to this effect, as it relates to companies, as pin action. It's a hot summer. Air conditioners sell well. Air conditioning manufacturers do well. Freon manufacturers do well. Parts manufacturers do well. And so forth…
This holds true at all levels of economic activity. Including the wealthy.
The wealthy do well. They buy stuff like, say, jewelry. The retailer does well. The wholesaler does well. The miners do well. All along this food chain people do well. Sales people,
managers, assemblers, miners, investors, et al do well, All have money to circulate, to spend.
The Socialist Democrats have demeaned this for decades as "trickle down economics." They do that to paint a picture, for the sake of winning, to justify pounding the rich. Not to promote truth. Disincentivize the rich from spending and you collapse the entire food chain.
All the rhetoric in the world won't stop the truths of pin action economics any more than it could stop an asteroid from striking the Earth.
Pin action economics is the reality and won't be denied.

Daily Obama Jokes 04/28/09

Daily Obama Jokes 04/28/09

What is Obama's position on illegal aliens?
They should return to their home planet.

Obama's Nursery Rhyme

Roses are red
Violets are blue
I love me
Why don't you?

The GM Proof
All agree. If Gm went out of business the effects
would be far reaching. GM employees would be
thrown out of work. Parts suppliers would
themselves be driven out of business. More
workers hitting the streets. City economies
collapsing. Businesses that depend on spending
from GM employees would whither. Their
suppliers would spiral down.
And on and on….
Pin action economics.
It's easy to see in the face of disaster. The effects
are rapid and undeniable. Plus the news media,
always thirsting for the misery of others, have
played it up endlessly.
What is less obvious is that pin action economics
built this chain. As GM grew so did the suppliers,
the cities, the businesses that served the people.
Pin action economics.
It works two ways.
And it is the dishonest rhetoric of "trickle down"
that deserves an unmarked grave.

Daily Obama Jokes 04/29/09

Daily Obama Jokes 04/29/09

As she went on a world junket how did Hillary travel?
Swine flew.

Why are voter turnouts so high in Chicago?
The homeless need the money.

Rich Pin Action

The last couple of columns pin action economics has been looked at in medium and large scale environs. The same thing happens as a result of wealth redistribution. An untold number of upscale services are provided to those that can afford them. Millions depend on this for their living, even the creation of their personal wealth. There are over 300 million of us. Hitting up the top 2% is like removing 6 million small businesses from the economy.
Not good.
Pin action on the upside builds across time. On the downside it is fast and devastating.
The proper way to build an economy is to put as many people as possible on can economic path swinging upwards. As people can afford more goods and services jobs are created and the society strengthens.
Socialism assumes stagnancy, sameness, a false equilibrium that ultimately drags down its victims.

It's PIN ACTION economics, not trickle down.

Daily Obama Jokes 04/30/09

Why do Democrats vote for higher taxes?
Why not? They don't pay them anyways.

Why are Chicago elections so honest?
Once voters get bought, they stay bought.

Chinese Stimulus

CNBC was interesting today. There was a good deal of talk in the afternoon on the Chinese stimulus bill. Caterpillar announced record orders from China. The Chinese want to build 30 nuclear reactors. That sent Shaw Group soaring. The overwhelming consensus was that the Chinese, spending less than we are, are doing far more to repair the world economy then the United States is with our stimulus bill. The Chinese, getting tired of our funny money, are stockpiling copper and other hard assets. They are spending more on telecom infrastructure alone than the entire amount of infrastructure spending for 2009 in our stimulus bill.
As a side note there was a blurb in Scientific American recently that the Department Of Energy has a viable plan for expanding our energy grid, upgrading it and it running coast to coast, at a cost of 60 billion dollars. The total infrastructure spending n the 800 billion stimulus bill is about 10% . Most of the stimulus bill gets spent in 2010, curiously an election year. Hmm. And the energy grid, which everyone agrees is badly in need of revamping, won't get the attention it needs.
We will, however, get social programs and paper shuffling
The Chinese are laying the groundwork for developing true wealth. We redistribute Monopoly money.
Which leads me to ask:
Why are the Communists in Washington and the

Capitalists in Beijing?
Daily Obama Jokes 05/01/09

What miracle did Obama perform to celebrate 100 days in office?
He made a blind man deaf.

Why did they spend $300,000 buzzing New York for a photo op?
No one got Obama Photoshop for Christmas.

Inflation Rising?

Long term bond yields are creeping up, a possible precursor to inflation. Thought I'd take a break from commentary to make some investment suggestions. I have small positions in each of these. Full disclosure and all that.

SLV
   An exchange traded fund follows the price of silver. Possibly undervalued in relation to gold, though all the precious metals will go up in an inflationary environment.

TBT
   An exchange traded fund that is double levered against the price of long term government bonds. As bond prices come down, this goes up. With long term bonds at around three per cent I just can't see much risk, but a lot of potential reward.

URE
   A double levered fund that tracks the real estate index. It's trading under $4 a share and was in the mid thirties only a year ago. If the commercial real estate defaults coming up are manageable this could win big in a 2-3 year time frame.

Daily Obama Jokes 05/02/09
Daily Obama Jokes 05/02/09

Conservatives raise kids.
Liberal Socialists raise other people's kids.

It got so cold this winter someone saw Obama with his hands in his own pockets.

Comrade Obama Saves The Day

Chrysler is in bankruptcy. Obama tried to screw the bondholders and they are fighting back.
Good for them.
Normally when a company goes into bankruptcy the bondholders come first. They have
risked their money to keep the company afloat. Seems fair.
The Obama proposal would give the workers (read UAW) 50% control of the company to offset the entitlements and handouts, er , excuse me, debts they are "owed." There was no risk taken in the occurring of these obligations, unlike bondholders.
Meanwhile union workers are griping because they will no longer get the Monday after Easter off.
Give me a break.
The bondholders took risk and deserve the lion's share of the settlement. If this doesn't occur it could mean trouble for the entire bond market. Why take a chance and loan a company money if the government is going to come in and screw you?
I haven't seen anyone bring this up yet but one of the tenets of communism is that workers should control production. Hmmm. Kind of like what Obama is proposing?
It sure looks like a backdoor route to communism

to me.
Obama is serving his union masters.
Obama is serving a communist ideal and the
discredited vision of Karl Marx.
He is not serving the people.

And remember
"its pin action economics, not trickle down!"

Daily Obama Jokes 05/03/09

A republican, a libertarian and a democrat were having lunch in a family restaurant one winter day when a bum with long hair and a scraggly beard came in and sat down at a corner table. The waitress walked by him several times, ignoring him,
"Excuse me," asked the conservative of his waitress, "but why are you ignoring that man?"
"Oh, he's one of the local homeless," replied the waitress. "He has no money and never orders anything, but the boss let's him come in to get warm."
"Well, get him some soup and a sandwich and put it on my bill," instructed the republican.
"And something to drink. Some milk perhaps," chimed in the libertarian.
"And pie for dessert," offered the liberal. "I'll cover that."
So the waitress brought all the food over to the homeless one, who ate heartily of it. When he was finished the homeless man came over to his benefactors and said, "I am Jesus, the Christ. You have given me food when I am hungry and drink for my thirst. I will reward for this." He placed his hand on the republican and said, "You have arthritis. It is gone and shall never bother you again."
Next he turned to the libertarian and placed his hand upon him. "You have migraine headaches. Never again will you suffer from a headache."
Finally he turned to the democrat.
"DON'T TOUCH ME!" screamed the democrat. "I'M ON DISABILITY!"

Finally A Bank Bill

For years the banks have been ripping people off via credit card policies. Finally the congress is taking some action. This is not a liberal or conservative issue. The banks have been equal opportunity opportunists.

What I am upset with is the heel dragging in congress (mixed with a healthy dose of lobbying, no doubt)

Before doing anything at all. The fact is that many of the tricks of the credit card companies could have been dealt with by legislation that would take less than a single piece of paper. No rocket science required.

Instead there have been months of committee meetings and deal making and such while a super bill is put together. One which leaves, by the way, some important areas untouched. In the meantime we, the people, have had to endure abuses and costs at the hands of the manipulative banks. Congress has cost you money by making simple problems complex.

The system has not been serving you. We need a methodology for submitting quick fixes directly to congress for rapid up and down votes. Perhaps a channel in which the president (though one shudders at the thought of what this president might think needs fixed) submits legislature directly to congress to fix simple things without a lot of power jockeying.

Tomorrow we start with some examples.

"It's pin action economics, not tickle down."

Daily Obama Jokes 05/04/09

Why don't they ever photograph Obama's best side?
He's sitting on it.

A union worker comes limping into the cafeteria on his lunch break.
"Hey," asked his buddy, "how come you're limping?"
"I think I've got a splinter in my foot."
"Why don't you take it out?"
"On my own time?"

Usury

Apparently unaddressed in this credit bill is the interest rate game the banks play.
Here's how it works:
Different states have different usury laws limiting the amount of interest that may be charged on loans of various sorts.
Banks set up their credit card operations in the highest interest states. In your credit card agreement you agree to be bound by the laws of that state. If you are in a lower interest state you have been screwed out of the protections of your state law. The Supreme Court has ruled this constitutional.
This is trash. Call me a bleeding heart conservative, but I am in favor of level and fair playing fields and against predatory practices.
This is predatory. What's worse, those that get clobbered are those who can afford it least. The poor working Joe. If you're rich you'll never see that max rate. If you're the guy on the street and get sick or have an emergency and are late on a payment you get jacked up to an interest rate over 30%.
This sure isn't the spirit of Christianity and forgiveness I grew up with.

We need a national usury law to prevent this kind of abuse. Say, prime plus 8%?
The legislation could be done on a single piece of paper.

"It's pin action economics, not trickle down!"

Daily Obama Jokes 05/05/09

When Barack was in college Satan appeared
before him in his dorm room one night.
Obama, studying at his desk, looked up, startled,
and asked, "What are you doing here, Satan?"
"I've come to offer you a deal," replied the Prince
Of Darkness. "I will make of you a great lawyer.
Then a leader of men, a great politician beloved
throughout the land. Millions will worship you as
the next messiah. And all the world will speak
your name with reverence. And all you have to
do is sell me your soul."
Obama thought for a minute. "Okay, I don't get
it. What's the catch?"

Why was Michelle so disappointed on her
wedding night?
Barack had 12 oysters and only 8 of them worked.

The Dating Game

Here's another piece of trash that banks do. I
don't think it's just deceptive, but, to my way of
thinking, fraudulent.
On your credit card statement you'll notice a
billing date. What happens when that date is on a
weekend or holiday? If so, you're credit card
company actually requires your payment to be
received and processed by the business day
preceding. By noon, if mailed, by 5pm if paid on
line or over the phone. On a holiday weekend this
can cut up to three days off your payment period.
Another way to generate fees and higher interest
rates while actually telling you an out and out lie.
I learned this the hard way. I went online to pay
a bill on a Saturday that was due on a Sunday.
The system kept telling me the bill would be
credited Monday. I called customer service. They
couldn't take my payment and credit it that day
either. The best I could do was complain loudly

enough that they waived the late fee.
Again, this could be corrected with a single page piece of legislation. No smoke and back rooms wheeling and dealing needed.

"It's pin action economics, not trickle down!"

Daily Obama Jokes 05/06/09

Obamanomics
Suckers should never be allowed to keep their
money.

It would be great if Obama were pope rather
than president. Then we'd only have to kiss his
ring.

The Interest Rate Trap

Credit card companies have the ability to modify
interest rates with sufficient notice. You, lucky
devil that you are, get a written notice of same
and have the right to cancel the card. Sounds fair,
but there is a catch. In order to cancel the card
you have to pay off any balance.
Of course, if you have a balance it's most likely
because you can't pay it off.
So you're stuck with the higher interest rate.
Gotcha!
This can be addressed by grandfathering
balances and any applicable interest accrued by
those balances at their original rate.
A one page piece of legislation.

"It's pin action economics, not trickle down!"

Daily Obama Jokes 05/07/09

The democratic candidate was glad handing the crowd and came upon a youngish man obviously just over voting age.
"Well, young man, may I count on your vote?"
"No, sir," replied the man. "I'm a republican."
"A republican!" snorted the democrat. "Why are you a republican?"
"Well. sir, my daddy was republican and his daddy before him. So I guess I'm a republican."
"And if you're daddy and grand daddy were horse thieves? What would that make you?"
"Well, I guess then I'd be a democrat."

Chicago Election Philosophy:
Vote early. Vote often.

I'm Offended! APOLOGISE!

I just hate it when some loony gets up and says this about anything. There is some assumption that there is an absolute standard by which offense is measured.
Not so.
Offense is always a personal choice. What one person finds offensive another finds true. There is no absolute.
You hear a statement. You compare it to your internal judgment data base and come to a variety of conclusions. One of those is whether or not something is offensive.
Let's take an example.
You hear someone from Nambla defend child pornography.
I am offended by child pornography. You are offended by child pornography. We choose to be offended.
But not everyone is offended by child pornography. That's why there is a thriving market for this trash throughout the world. There

56

are enough creeps, my value judgment, around to make that market.

The fact is that "I'm offended!" is often used as a power ploy. Political enemies and social rival groups use it all the time to try and seize a moral high ground. It's not really about offense, or right or wrong.

It's about winning.

About power.

And if I say something that offends someone? The chip is on their shoulder. They can deal with it.

Socialist Democrat: Someone who believes it's okay to kill unborn babies but wrong to waterboard people who want to kill us.

Daily Obama Jokes 05/08/09

What did Obama reply when he was accused of
being pretentious?
"Moi?"

"I'm glad Obama's president. But then again, I'm
a comedian"

The Stress Test

I'm not so sure I'm buying this government
stress test of banks. Ever since Paulson the
government has been trying to gain control of
private business. Banks aren't allowed to pay
back tarp money and instead have to deal
with onerous government oversight. The attempt
to mutually take over control of Chrysler by the
feds and unions combined at the expense of
bondholders and hundreds of years of
accepted bankruptcy law. Obama's wanting to
now dominate the student lending arena.
You get the picture.
Let's take Well Fargo. The government says they
need more capital. More government strings
attached loans? Conversion of government held
preferred stock to common, giving more power to
the government (while losing the nice dividend
the tax payers are at least collecting on the
preferred)?
Hmmm.
Warren Buffet holds a nice sized stake in Wells
Fargo. This past weekend he stated on
nationwide television that Wells was the
strongest of the banks and was in fine shape.
Something isn't jiving here.
At least the word is Wells will sell more stock.
But the question is are we to believe the profit
motivated Buffet who has his own money at
stake or a power hungry government that for

months has been seeking to invade the private sector with unprecedented hubris?
Call me skeptical but I just can't trust what this government says.

You may be a Socialist Democrat if you believe businesses create oppression and governments create prosperity.

"It's pin action economics, not trickle down

Daily Obama Jokes 05/09/09

Capital punishment means never having to say ,"What? You again?"

Politicians who fail to learn from history doom the rest of us to repeat it.

Viva Montana!

If you missed the Glenn Beck Show on Thursday 05/08 you need to try and find it online or get it from a friend. Very substantial and interesting.. Montana recently fought back against Federal intrusion. They passed a law denying the Federal government the ability to regulate guns made in Montana and kept in Montana. The argument is that the Feds may have the authority to regulate interstate commerce, but if the gun never leaves the state it has no authority. Interesting.
Texas is passing similar, even tougher regulation. I'm pleased to see someone is fighting back constructively against the Washington power grab. Be nice to see Obama Hood and his Merry Dems get a good spanking.
You can expect this to go to the Supremes.
That's the really scary part.
The Imperial Obamancy rolls along. His majesty has requested 17 million in spending cuts from the up coming budget. Out of 3 trillion, that's all he could find! And what did he find?
Hmmm.
Well, he wants to cut a federal death benefit program for police officers from 110 million to 60 million. Plenty of money laying around for people who don't work, though.
His Obamancy loves unions. Perhaps he should be hearing loudly from the law enforcement brotherhoods. On this and on other things as well.

Socialist Democrats believe Americans with guns are more of a threat than a nuclear armed North Korea or Iran.

Daily Obama Jokes 05/10/09

Government wants to control everything!
Get Your Protest Permit Now!

How do union fairy tales begin?
"One upon a time and a half...."

"Got Hate?"

The Democratic Socialists love to accuse other
people of hate. "If you disagree with me you are
full of hate! You hate blacks! You hate Hispanics!
You hate Gays! '
Blah! Blah! Blah!
It's all rhetoric for the purpose of winning, of
course. Most of the hatred I see on the political
flows like blood from a ripped artery out of the
left. Listen to the Keith Uberman Comedy Hour
on MSNBC. Just once. One hour. Try being a
conservative speaker at a university. Hope you
like coconut cream. Look at the media coverage
of the tea parties, at the scorn heaped
upon loyal Americans by an agenda driven elite.
How would the media react if it were half naked
gay activists prancing for their cause du jour?
Wouldn't it be nice if the conservatives got equal
treatment from the media?
"They disagree with me! They must be ignorant
rubes! Hate mongers! Let's not listen to them!
Let's stomp them!"
As soon as they can't deal with the issues the
emotionally charged accusations and belligerent
obfuscations begin.
Here's the thing to keep in mind when this starts:
As soon as the name calling begins the liberal
has run out of ammunition. "The argument has
been lost, It's time to get out the sticks and beat
our way to victory."
It's time to cut their mike.

Socialist Democrats believe that the same teacher that can't teach your kids to read is qualified to teach them sex education.

Daily Obama Jokes 05/11/09

His Obaminess is now proposing a National
Beverage.
Kool-Aid

You're walking along the Potomac River. Harry
Reid and Queen Pelosi have fallen in and are
drowning. You only have time to save one. What
do you do?
Go to lunch.

Hate! Hate! Hate!

You may recall a few days back that I discussed
offensiveness and believed taking offense is
always a choice?
Today I choose to be officially offended by the
hate rhetoric and accusations of the left. Instead
of dealing with things on the level of facts and
ideas the socialists simply ascribe a derogatory
motive to their opponents and attack. So called
social liberals are, in fact, amongst the most
closed minded people I've ever seen.
Let's take that giant of liberal intellectualism,
Janine Garofalo. She was a few weeks back all
over the media proclaiming that anyone who
doesn't support Barack Obama is a racist who
hates having a black man in the White House..
It is, of course, inconceivable that anyone could
disagree with his doctrines, polices, actions,
philosophies or demeanor.
Nope, all that is self evidently beyond question.
Can anyone, even a socialist democrat, believe
this crap?
One has the right of free speech, of course. But
no one is obligated to listen. Until Socialist
Democrats want to come and joust in the arena
of ideas the sub intellectual bomb throwers
should be delegated to the schoolyard by all (not

just conservatives but by middle Dems
and independents as well).
Name calling is never truth.

 Socialist Democrats belief that global warming
is not caused by cyclical factors but is the fault
of hockey moms driving SUVs.

Daily Obama Jokes 05/12/09

Did you hear about Obama's accident?
He was out for his morning walk and got hit by a
speed boat.

Why doesn't Queen Pelosi bake chocolate chip
cookies?
It's too hard to peel the M&Ms..

A Profile Of Hate.

Witless talking heads keep spouting off that
people who don't like Obama must be racist
haters of blacks. This is of course stereotyping,
and just as intellectually vapid as, say, the
rantings of the Ku Klux Klan. In essence, they are
no different. Just the target changes.
Just for fun, let's look take a close look at one of
these "racists."
Me!
I disagree on almost everything Obama stands
for. According to the stereotyping, bigoted liberal
media machine, I must be a racist. Let's look at
my history and get a firm understanding of my
racist roots.
I grew up in a Jewish neighborhood. As the
Christian kid I was the odd one out. Funny ,
though. I was never picked on or denigrated for
being different. You were that. I was this. No big
deal. Let's play Monopoly.
Hmm.
I attended Cleveland State University. It's an
urban college with a widely diverse student
body. Had whites, blacks, ex-military, liberal,
conservatives, foreigners, fraternity Greeks,
computer geeks. You name it.
Not exactly a hotbed of intolerance.
Must be work. My first job was as a cashier at a
Sears auto center. Working my way through
school, mostly. (no suck 'em into the system

student loans back then.). The store was located at 86th and Euclid, right in the heart of the inner city black community. Spent over 7 years there. My coworkers ranged from hillbillies from West Virginia to black gospel music group leaders. 99% of our customers were black and I got to deal with them on an everyday life basis. Chatted with many as they waited for a repair to be done. What I learned was simple: There are good black people and there are bad black people. There are smart black people and not so smart black people. There are black people all along the curve.

Nope, doesn't seem to be a trigger for racism there.

Perhaps it's my neighborhood that makes me such a racist that I disagree with Obama. Let's see. I live on a short street with about ten houses. One is vacant and been for sale for a couple years. Another gets rented to college students 10 months of the year. The two families to the right of my house are young black families with little kids. Across the street is a black family, an older, black single man, one old European immigrant family and a young couple from India who have kids plus their mom living with them. Then there is my family. My wife is Jewish. That makes my eldest son, who is autistic, half Jewish half Wasp. My other son is adopted from Guatemala and is part Indian, part Hispanic. There's only one full blooded Wasp on the street. Me.

If I were a racist I think I'd be somewhere else living a different life.

The true bigots, based along political lines rather than ethnic, are the media elite. They propagate stereotyping , scorn, and division. Their way or the highway. A Nationalist Socialist propaganda machine under construction.

Be Afraid. Be Very Afraid!

Daily Obama Jokes 05/13/09

Why do hookers vote for liberals?
They don't care who gets in.

What do you call it when you catch a union
worker sleeping on the job?
Overtime.

That Didn't Take Long

Arlen Specter's new friends, the democrats, have
already screwed him over. Before switching
parties (again) Harry Reid promised Specter he
wouldn't lose any seniority.
Whoops.
Arlen, at 79, now finds himself the junior senator
on all his committees.
He's lucky. So far they've only stuck in the knife.
They haven't twisted.
Remember Queen Pelosi denying knowing about
the water boarding? Thanks to a Freedom
Of Information Act request transcripts of her
meetings on the subject it seems she had
full knowledge of what was going on as early as
2004.
Anyone on MSNBC happen to mention this? Lead
story on the Keith Uberman Comedy Hour
perhaps? I refuse to watch MSNBC anymore, but
I want to be fair. If so, let me know
I'm really fed up with liberals wanting to act like
their poop is chocolate ice cream.
Any way we can trade these guys to Iran for a
couple of terrorists to be named later? We'd be
better off.

Socialist Democrat: Someone who thinks gender
roles are indoctrination and that gay lifestyles
should be promoted in public schools.

Daily Obama Jokes 05/14/09

Some liberals are rude and arrogant. But others are just the opposite.
Arrogant and rude.

Liberals are now marketing a new stealth camouflage condom
You never see them coming....

Word Play

One of the problems we have in politics is that we have our nomenclature backwards.
I'm thinking especially of the terms "Liberal" and "Conservative."
Liberals believe:

Everything should be controlled.

Schools should be used as a means of social indoctrination
Enemies should be shouted down and personally destroyed
The state is the source of all good things
It's not your money, the state just let's you use it.
Wealth is a bad thing.
People are owed various things by the world.
Religion needs to be subjugated to the state.

I could go on, but you get the idea. Doesn't seem to be very liberating to me.

Conservatives believe:
Honest capitalism is good.
Innovation and creativity are sparked in an atmosphere of freedom and with the nurturing of ideas.
Money motivates.
Values flow from religion. The state should be created by the flow of morals, not the

state   determining the values and morals.
Honesty, integrity and trust are paramount to the
functioning of a free society.
Tolerance of differences within nondestructive
parameters of behavior is desirable.
 Personal achievement leads to true self esteem
based on accomplishment.

Again, I could go on. Seems a lot freer than the
ideas of the liberals.

I do believe that part of our problems are based
on lies inherent in the labels we've chosen. The
connotations these words have come to possess
do not reflect the reality of the named. Liberal is
not free. Conservative is not repressive, stagnant
or old fashioned.
Note also that I do not use the terms republican
or democrat.
I say conservatives should hijack the term liberal
from the left as an exercise an intellectual
honesty.

 Socialist Democrats believe you should be
working for the state, not the state working for
you.

Daily Obama Jokes 05/15/09

Queen Pelosi's husband walked into a jewelry store shortly before Christmas.
"I want to smother my wife in diamonds!" he announced.
"Gee," replied the clerk, 'there must be a cheaper way..."

Three Chicago council members, a republican, an independent, and a democrat, were sentenced to 5 years in prison for corruption. Each was allowed to take one luxury item with him. The republican took law books. The independent took medical books. The democrat took 200 cartons of cigarettes.
5 years later, just before they were to be released, the warden called them into his office.
"What to you plan to do when you get out of here?" he asked.
"I'm going to become a lawyer," replied the republican.
"I'm going to become a doctor," replied the independent.
"I'm going to find some matches," replies the democrat.

Hang On Tight

The tax avalanche is about to begin.
On the table is a proposal to start taxing your health benefits.
You making under 250k? You'll be taxed.
Remember that campaign promise by His Obaminess? You didn't drink that Kool-Aid, I hope. If you did, don't worry. You get a do over in 2012.
And the new sin tax will be on food. A national tax on soft drinks. Salty stuff like potato chips. Fatty foods, like the stuff you get at your

bakery. Perhaps the cupcakes you bake in your home. And, of course, more taxes on DEMON ALCOHOL. The cost of beer and chips and a game on the telly will be going up, sports fans.

The food Nazis must be in heaven.

These are all also regressive taxes. The less you make the more you hurt. Obama, friend of the poor…

You make less than 250k?

You'll be taxed. Oops, there goes that promise again.

Oh, and about that promise. It seems that was before deductions. The real number is now 235k. And I bet it drops some more.

On the brighter side His Obaminess has announced that there are no plans to place a national tax on Vaseline.

I predict it's only a matter of time until he comes after your 401Ks and IRAs as well. In a way, he already is. People needing money have been pulling out record sums from their 401Ks.

Taxable with a 10% penalty.

Make everything too costly. Destroy the economy. Start a stampede. Collect the tax and penalty.

Just because you're paranoid doesn't mean they aren't out to get you.

Democratic Socialists believe that all money is the property of the government, which you are allowed to use from it time to time.

Daily Obama Jokes 05/16/09

What is Queen Pelosi's recipe for chicken soup?
First you bring the Perrier to a boil....

Obama has announced his latest social innovation.
Drive through soup kitchens.

To Regulate

Most of us don't realize that much of the federal
government's usurped power comes from the
interpretation of a single word.
Regulate.
The Constitution grants congress the power to
regulate commerce amongst the several states.
Today we think of regulations and rules and
agencies that oversee everything under the sun.
This authority comes from that single word
regarding interstate commerce. If it can be
construed as being or affecting such commerce
congress leaps to get its finger in the pie. And
we've been conditioned to accept it.
It wasn't always so.
Our forefathers intended regulate in the meaning
"to make regular." An analogy would be a
pacemaker, which regulates one's heartbeat.
Such was the case for over 100 years.
Then came a case involving one single, solitary
farmer who was engaging in some activities the
feds didn't like. The Supremes didn't either. In a
decision that was controversial at the time the
court granted congress the authority it sought.
And the flood gates opened.
It's time to take back our country and once again
delimit the power of the federal government. If
2/3 of the states agree a new continental
congress can be convened and the constitution
changed and/or clarified. The feds have trampled
on the states and the citizenry for years and now
is the time for them to unite and fight back.

While we still can.

Democratic Socialists believe that it's okay for the president to be against gay marriage, that a beauty queen who states the same position should be castigated.

Daily Obama Jokes 05/17/09

He that robs Peter to pay Paul may rest assured
he has Paul's vote.

Rev. Wright was wandering a part of Chicago he
was unfamiliar with. One of his church members
had an accident at work and had been taken to a
local hospital, but the Rev had trouble finding it.
As it happened along came Barack Obama.
"Hey, Barack," called Rev. Wright, "what's the
fastest way to the hospital?"
So Obama threw him under a bus.

Honesty Gets Trashed

So Sarah Palin is writing a book. Actually, she is
collaborating on a book, which means a
professional author will be setting her history,
thoughts and ideas on paper.
Perfectly normal. Happens all the time.
Of course, the leftist media is howling. "She can't
read a book! She can't write a book! She needs
help!"
Attack dogs like that Chris Mathews serve up
heaping helpings of scorn and ridicule.
Truth.
Most famous people don't write their own books.
Ghost writing is a time honored profession and a
publishing essential.
Having self published a little book on life with my
autistic son I will tell you that the process is time
consuming. Organizing and outlining the book,
getting it down on paper, rewriting, searching out
typos, and then doing it all again. It's quite time
consuming.
Sarah Palin's primary job is running the state of
Alaska. I seriously doubt, based on my own
experience, that she has the actual time to
devote to writing the book. As a result she'll work
with a pro.

As I mentioned, this is a regular occurrence in this business.

Raise your hand if you believe every book written by famous people is actually written by that person.

So what s Palin's sin?

Being honest about how the book s being written. And once again we see that the liberal media has no interest in doing anything but winning, but controlling what the populace thinks.

Daily Obama Jokes 05/18/09

Obama always wants to have the last word.
I just wish he'd get to it.

Congress
The world's only cathouse that loses money.

The Fundamental Right

It seems to me that the constitution was
based on a single, fundamental right, unstated
and unsung. To be sure the constitution
guarantees a variety of specific rights (at least
until the congress and/or courts can connive to
take them away).
We have the right of free speech (unless you're
protesting an abortion clinic or haven't got the
requisite permits), The right to vote (in some
places, several times), the right to bear arms (as
long as you comply with arcane and convoluted
regulations) .
But these rights and others are not fundamental.
Rather they flow from the single fundamental
right.
That right is simply the right of the citizens to be
free of an overly oppressive and controlling
government.
At the time of the revolution George the 3rd was
running everything he could. His enemies were
thrown in prison, he taxed everything he could
think of, and even ran the church in
England. British troops marched our streets,
making sure his dictates were followed.
It is in this environment that the states rebelled.
To cast off an oppressive and controlling
government.
We fought to break those shackles, to make the
citizen the master.
And we have lost our way.

Socialist Democrats believe that religious charities are undeserving of public support but that bloated and expensive government monopolies shoud redistribute wealth.

Daily Obama Jokes 05/19/09

Obamanomics
Rob the rich
Pay off the poor
'Til there are no
Rich anymore

What do socialist agendas and used cars have in common?
They both have a tendency to backfire.

The Constitution's Function

If the underlying right we share is the right to be free of an oppressive government, what, then, is the function of the Constitution?
True, the document, as originally written accomplished many functions. It divides powers between the states and the Federal government. Specifically, and oft ignored, the federal government is granted certain powers and those powers only. If a power is not granted then it is not possessed by the federal government. Period. The Constitution divides the federal government into three branches, in theory making it difficult for an oppressive state to arise.
To further insure its goals specific rights of the citizenry were delineated. Government at no level was to have the power to breach those rights.
All these things done by the Constitution served a fundamental purpose: to limit the power of the government. I can't say this too strongly. Limiting the power of government was, indeed, the original function of our Constitution. All the sections and clauses within are merely the framework, the tools by which this done.
Regretfully, just as misers are greedy for money, politicians are greedy for power. And so end runs have come into play. Ill-advised amendments granting unlimited authorities, such as the

government's unlimited power to tax. Reinterpretations of phrases or meanings of words that have nothing to do with their original intent. The false claim that the document is a living document by control freak ideologues seeking to impose their will and control over society. Worst of all, the Constitution is under attack by internationalists who would subjugate us to the whims of the world community.

The time has come to cut the government down to size. The only way to assure this is to have the states call for the convening of a new constitutional congress. If 2/3 of the state legislatures agree, this can be done. This is the surest way to undo the damage that has decimated our freedom.

 Democratic Socialists believe judges in third world countries have more right to shape our legal decisions than our own people do.

Daily Obama Jokes 05/20/09

What's the difference between a liberal and a savings bond?
Bonds mature.

What was Queen Pelosi before she ran for congress?
A female impersonator.

We really need to convene a new Continental Congress to clarify and redefine the constitution. Misinterpretations abound in our society and new issues unforeseen in 1776 have arisen. Let's look at some examples.

Taxation
When the amendment was passed to allow the congress to tax income there were no limitations placed on this power. Our fearless leaders have gone hog wild and need reined in.

Regulation of interstate commerce
The term regulate meant to make regular when the Constitution was written. Thanks to a 1940's Supreme Court ruling the congress uses this clause to try and control everything. Again, the government needs reined in.

Abortion
There will never be an agreement on this issue. It could be thrown out of the national spotlight, though, by making it a state's rights determination. Let the locals decide for their state. The worst that happens for the pro abortion lobby is that an abortion becomes a bus ticket more expensive. Let liberals start a foundation to cover the cost, if they want.

Gun control.
Again, recent attempts to redefine the words

used in the Constitution to grant this right have led to some silly arguments. If only a militia were meant to bear arms then why did this go unnoticed and unenforced for nearly 2 centuries? Again, the states need to assert their authority.

Separation of church and state
Lots of silliness here, too. Especially when one considers that a lot of the anti religion crowd bases their thoughts on a single line in a letter by Thomas Jefferson. Simple is best. The state should not control any church. No church should control any state. Nothing more. Nothing less. That's how I read the Constitution. Clarifying this would once again allow cities to lease facilities to the Boy Scouts and such . And public buildings could have Christmas and Channukah decorations again!

Redefine citizen requirements.
Currently we are one of only a handful of nations that grants citizenship solely based on birth within the national border. This is causing all kinds of problems when illegal aliens enter the country and give birth. Now the child is a citizen and the parents are not, ,leading to major problems. The children of illegal aliens should not be granted automatic citizenship.

A national language
Something that should be addressed, if only because it has become a subject of some conversation. I say no. The purpose of the Constitution should be to keep the people free from oppression and limit the government. While I like the idea, it would be a misuse of Constitutional intent to mandate such here.

Term limits.
Politicians in power too long become more concerned with their personal power, with

getting reelected, than the people they serve. 5 terms for a congressman and 2 terms for a senator seem about right.

Flag burning
Some have wanted to address this in the Constitution and make it illegal. Seems like free speech to me and again the purpose of the Constitution should be to limit government.

Gay marriage
Much as I oppose this, it should not be a Constitutional issue, unless someone can make a case for such an amendment limiting government.

I'm sure we could come up with more issues to discuss. The lack of clarity on all the above should be sufficient to convince anyone that we need to convene a new Continental Congress to clarify these issues. It actually could be done quite simply. It only requires the legislatures of 2/3 of the states to vote to convene to begin the process. What we need is a grass roots movement to get that fire lit.

Socialist Democrats believe kids should be given condoms instead of a sense of responsibility.

Daily Obama Jokes 05/21/09

What's the difference between an audience with the Queen of England and Obama?
You only have to go down on one knee for the Queen.

What's the difference between a dead liberal in the middle of the road and a dead snake in the middle of the road?
There are skid marks in front of the snake.

There's a section of law that has been used to screw you, the public. A few years back congress passed a twenty year extension of the copyright protections, bringing work for hire protections up to 99 years. This basically denies you, the public, access to use characters and works from years gone by. I refer to this as the Mickey Mouse law as it was passed shortly before Mickey would have entered the public domain. Have to repay Hollywood for its liberal support somehow, eh? Admittedly, this does not affect most people. Most of us aren't interested in, say, making our own cartoons. It is important in this regard: it is one more example of congress reining in your freedoms and what is, traditionally yours. The only thing it does is extend the ability of certain corporations and special interests to continue to make money. In some instances it denies the public access to a work altogether.
One example is the movie "Porgy And Bess". Haven't seen this classic on Turner Classic Movies or AMC, have you? The rights holder has chosen not to release this film, for whatever reason, for the public to see. It's not been aired in decades and it isn't available on dvd or video. Anyone who has ever wanted to own a copy of the movie or see it, either again or for the first time, is denied the opportunity.

Let me be very clear here. The rights holder is well within his rights.

However, under the old law, the film would eventually enter the public domain. Any film collector with a print of the film would be able to bring to the public in any of a variety of formats. Under new law it remains under wraps for an additional 20 years.

The creative world is further stifled in its ability to use fictional characters. Let's take Sherlock Holmes, for example. He passed into the public domain years ago. As a result his fandom, which s quite large, has been able to expand his fictional canon considerably. New stories and novels appear about Holmes all the time The ability of his legions to keep the character fresh has no doubt gone a long way in maintaining his ongoing popularity.

The same is true of Bram Stoker's Dracula.

This won't be possible with, say, Indiana Jones, for an additional 20 years.

There are a plethora of characters and films of relatively minor importance to the general public, but of great interest to collectors and fans. Oft times films are considered too small to merit the efforts of a release by a studio controlling the rights. So they languish on a dusty shelf.

The public domain exists in part so that arts and performances are not lost to we the people.

This expansion of the law in no way serves the public interest and is merely another example of government putting the desires of special interests ahead of the rest of us.

Socialist Democrats think that all blacks should vote alike and that any who vote Republican are "Uncle Toms."

Daily Obama Jokes 05/22/09

What do the Washington Redskins get for a safety?
A condom. Vulcanized.

Why was Bill Clinton's the least sexist administration in history?
Women filled hundreds of positions under Clinton.

The Song Remains The Same

Seems Obama Hood is rolling right along. CNBC today gave some details on the plan for GM. His Obaminess & Co will be tossing 39% of GM to the UAW. Bondholders, you know, those people who took risk to try and keep GM alive, will get about a 10% equity stake.
A demonstration of sorts was held in Washington by individuals who hold Gm bonds. Not hedge funds or speculators or investment bankers. We're talking Mom & Pop America. Mainly old folks who had invested money n these bonds, many for retirement. CNBC showed comments being made by 3-4. There were among them Obama supporters who now felt betrayed. Many were scared of losing their entire investment. Obama cowed the Chrysler bondholders. He gave speeches and public spankings blaming greedy hedge funds (it's greedy to want your money back?) for standing in the way of his wheeling and dealing. And eventually the bondholders folded.
Now we see more clearly that Obama is destroying the wealth of ordinary people, oft older folk with no time left to recover from his financial devastation, in order to turn companies over to the UAW. A Communist ideal is for the workers to control production. His Obaminess seems right on course.

And in the wake lives are being ruined and hundreds of years of bankruptcy law is being tossed aside.

There is one thing to look forward to. The UAW used to strong arm, er, negotiate with the auto companies. Now they will, for all practical purposes, be the company.

It will be fun to watch when they negotiate themselves.

And if you disagree with me, then you, Sir, are worse than Carter.

Socialist Democrats believe free speech is great, unless you disagree with them.

Daily Obama Jokes 05/23/09

Queen Pelosi and her husband were driving along the highway. They passed a billboard of a beautiful young woman drinking a name brand can of beer.
"I suppose if I drank 5 cans of that stuff I'd look like that," mused Queen Pelosi.
"No," replied her husband. "If I drank 5 cans of beer, THEN you'd look like that."

In Chicago, it's not the voting that matters. It's the counting.

Obama, The Victim

His Obaminess seems to be developing a blame Bush strategy for answering critics on the left. He's been blaming Bush for the economic situation (rightfully it's the SEC and congress combined). Yesterday, after trumpeting the closing of Gitmo a short while back, he announced that some dangerous people would be kept in permanent detention. When pressed by some disappointed journalists Obama said that he didn't create the situation, his predecessor did. Blame Bush. We seem to be getting the victim card here. In Socialist Victimology one is never responsible for anything bad that happens. It's always some one else. "What could I do? I'm just the victim here."
It's the message the president has sent several times.
"I AM A VICTIM."
A real leader takes ownership of a problem, picks a course of action, stands by it and defends it until such time as it succeeds or proves unviable. If it proves unviable, he admits his error and changes course.
Obama has quietly adopted a number of Bush positions. When called on it by the leftist media,

like a whiney little kid on a playground, the Prez
has dodged with, "Don't blame me. He started
it!"
And that is neither integrity nor leadership.

And if you disagree with me then you, Sir, are
worse than Stalin.

Socialist Democrats think the right of free speech
means a right of venue and that they should
therefore get unearned radio air time and the
expense of those who have proven worthy of it.

Daily Obama Jokes 05/24/09

An aide went up to Rangel and informed him,
" Bob Rogers just died. We'd like to get a little
something for his widow."
Okay, " replied Rangel. "I'll bid $14."

What will Obama do if we lose our AAA rating?
Find a different auto club.

Arrrgh!

It never ceases to amaze me how weird the
liberal commentary can get. On the news Friday
were reports that liberal bloggers were blaming
conservatives for Kris Allen winning American
Idol.
Huh?
Seems conservatives are all upset about Obama
winning. Seems we're supposed to be
homophobic and Adam Lambert wears make up
and all (kind of like them there Kiss fellas that
were on the show. Anyone want to call Gene
Simmons gay?). So conservatives all got together
and conspired and arranged massive dialing to
prevent Adam from winning. OUR REVENGE IS
COMPLETE!
Hmmm.
For the record, I thought Adam should have won.
But….. I thought his song choice, spooky and
weird, for his opening number was a mistake. He
should have brought it home with "Whole Lotta
Love." And who exactly says he's gay? He's in
show business. Make up like his is a gimmick, a
style. Has nothing to do with gender orientation.
Or have I missed something about Alice Cooper?
Quite frankly conservatives have far better things
to do than engage in a silly conspiracy like this.
And some liberal bloggers have far too much
time on their hands.

And if you disagree with me, then you, Sir, are worse than Idi Amin.

Socialist Democrats believe that when they lose an election it's because the voters didn't really understand the situation.

Daily Obama Jokes 05/25/09

Memorial Day

May those who protect us be blessed.

May those who have gone before smile down upon us from the gates of heaven

Daily Obama Jokes 05/26/09

What does Obama do when he comes to a fork in a road?
Go both ways.

How many pall bearers do they need at the funeral of a Chicago politician?
One, to slam the trunk.

It's So Funny...

Congress is a laugh riot. This week they wanted to pass a 900+ page bill that no one had read. The republicans, wanting to throw up a stumbling block, wanted to enforce a rule requiring the bill be read before congress, a feat that would take a normal person days. So the Dems hired a speed reader to read the bill ....
Let's all sing along now.
M-I-C
K-E-Y
While all this is funny on the outside, it brings up some serious issues. How on earth did this bill get to be over 900 pages long? You know it can't be on just one subject. Guys in the backrooms had to be horse-trading to get their own little pet pieces of blarney inserted. Makes me want to insert something myself.
And why are things being voted on that no one has read? Is this really about us? Or is it about winning? Just getting one's way?
Bills should be short and sweet and devoted to a single topic. Two at most. Not only does this horns waggling lead to endless crap getting passed it is time consuming and eats away resources that could be used getting real work done.
Back in 1952 congress passed the infrastructure legislation that led to our highway system. It's length? 29 pages.

Perhaps we need a movement next election. No votes for democrats. No votes for republicans. Get them all out and get in a bunch of independents and small party guys.

And if you disagree with me, then you, Sir, are worse than Fluffy McNutter.

Socialist Democrats believe that acceptable discussion tactics include talking over their opponents so they can't be heard.

Daily Obama Jokes 05/27/09

How many terrorists does it take to blow up a light bulb?
None. Terrorists don't blow, they suck.

John Kerry was going hunting and arrived at the lodge. After checking in the lodge owner asked him if he'd like any hunting dogs. "Sure," agreed Kerry and soon he was off to the woods with a couple of hounds.
A few hours later Kerry entered the lodge again. "How's the hunting?" asked the owner.
"Great!" replied Kerry. "Got any more dogs?"

Protecting What?

This last week His Obaminess was all over the news, vowing to protect "the American people and their values..."
Huh?
Superficially this sounds good, but it degenerates into more self serving rhetoric. Inherent in his statement is that a course of action can not be undertaken unless it both protects Americans and "their Values." Well, what are these values? Ask 300 million people and you'll get hundreds, thousands of differing answers. No one from the government has bothered to send me a questionnaire on what my values are. Perhaps we should send such a questionnaire to every adult in the country and establish some kind of curve or baseline. Obama Hood and his Merry Dems should love that idea. Expand government, more spending.
The real problem here is that Obama can't really know what our "values" are. We don't have one set of values. Therefore the values that he protects will be his own, projected on all of us. So what would he authorize if we captured a terrorist and learned there was a bomb set to go

95

off within the hour at an American School? What do we use? Harsh language?
How about if his own kids were at that school? Now do we break out the car battery and jumper cables?
Slime oozes from the lips of our fearless leader again, I fear.

And if you disagree with me, then you, Sir, are worse than Janeane Garofalo.

Daily Obama Jokes 05/28/09

Why don't they serve oatmeal at Gitmo?
It would be gruel and unusual punishment.

Why does Obama tax the rich?
The poor don't have any money.

Not A Living Document

Much discussion has gone on over whether the Constitution is a living document. Usually those who think so are the same crowd who want to control society by legislative, judicial or executive fiat.
The Constitution is not a living document.
The best proof is the Constitution itself. It is very difficult to change the Constitution. It requires congress and 2/3 of the states to agree to a change. If it were meant to be responsive to the whims of the moment a simple majority would suffice.
Stop also to consider the fact that much of the document is designed to protect the rights of minority groups (and I don't mean race. I mean any group that is a minority.) from the majority. One of the great dangers of democracy is that, in a pure and uncontrolled form, it can become the tyranny of the minority by the majority. Our forefathers foresaw this and protected us against such tyranny. Reducing the Constitution to a "living document" only reintroduces the danger.

And if you disagree with me, then you, Sir, are worse than Lex Luthor.

Socialist Democrats believe the Constitution says whatever they think it says.

Daily Obama Jokes 05/29/09

What happens when Obama goes bowling?
It's so quiet you can hear a pin drop.

From crooked folks mighty ACORNS grow.

The details of Government Motors fate are starting to clarify. The government will end up with 70% of the company, the UAW 20%, the secured bondholders 10% and possibly about 1% will be sucked out of those numbers for the current shareholders. We've already dumped 20 billion into the company. This move will cost another 50 billion or more additional.
Forget the fact that the secured bondholders have been shafted.
Forget the fact that the entire canon of bankruptcy law has been circumvented.
Forget the fact that this is another move toward fascism.
What I want to ask is why are we buying one of the worst, poorly run, nonperforming assets in the country? With 50 billion dollars there are any number of well run, profitable businesses we the people could buy into. Profit for the federal coffers. Profit that could be used to lower taxes, fund social security or rebuild infrastructure. Mind you. I in no way advocate the government buying companies, but if we must, then why this one?
Perhaps it's because GM provides a unique inroad into American society. Obama knows what kind of cars "America needs." Perhaps it's because it provides a means to expand control of society. Perhaps because it's an opportunity to impose little green cars on the country. Little things big guys like me couldn't get into with a barrel of bear grease and a crowbar.
Barack Obama.
Would you buy a new car from this man?

And if you disagree with me, then you, Sir, are worse than MSNBC.

Socialist Democrats think it's great to use untold numbers of acres for chasing windmills while ignoring the development of clean hybrid reactors with a small footprint.

Daily Obama Jokes 05/30/09

Why does Obama like living at the White House?
It has a big pool for his morning stroll.

When you don't vote you get bad government.
When you do vote you get bad government and
jury duty.

Hang On!

The government announced it took in 35% less in
taxes year over year in April. That's not good. For
us. Not only is the government spending money
it doesn't have, it's spending money it isn't going
to get. The shortfalls are widening.
The government will, of course, want to get back
what it thinks is its due. What options does it
have?
It can raise taxes.
This will be the first choice, of course. Never
mind that it will tank the economy by
demolishing economic activity.
It can begin hyper inflating the currency.
They'll try and avoid this one, The public will feel
this quickly and howl. But in the long run will
there be a choice?
With no visible means of support it can try
borrowing.
And just how dumb do we think the rest of the
world is? Just how much money does the rest of
the world have for us to devour anyways?
It could stiff everybody.
There are no bankruptcy courts for countries. We
could just default. Interest rates would soar and
world economic activity would suffer cardiac
arrest.
We could curtail our spending.
What? And interfere with our endless march
toward National Socialism? Fat chance.
With the last option most likely out of the running

all I can say is hang onto your hats, boys and girls. It's going to turn into a wild and bumpy ride.

And if you disagree with me then you, Sir, are worse than Himmler.

Socialist Democrats believe that you get to spend money raising your children for the benefit of the state.

daily Obama Jokes 05/31/09

Why is Obama able to laugh at himself?
Why not? Everybody else does.

Save your money. It might be worth something someday.

Wage Slaves

It came out this week that the government debt is now over $550,000 per household. Bear in mind that government debt is your debt. Somehow that money has to be sucked out of your pocket.
The portion that you are now allowed to keep after taxes is exactly that. Our "leaders" can come in and vote to take whatever they want whenever they want. You are wage slaves to the spending behemoth that both parties have put into place. You think you're working for yourself? Think again.
And don't think your retirement accounts are safe. Your 401Ks and IRAs represent a huge pool of money the government hasn't hit on. Many of you have saved diligently. Others have little or nothing put aside for whatever reason.
I can see it now.
"It's not fair that you should have so much, " whine the Socialist Democrats. "You should share. Here, let's put this gun to your head and help."
Never mind that you worked and saved and invested. Fair, to them, isn't based on reward for what you've done. It's based on what you have. And when you have more, you become a target.
I wouldn't expect to see this unless Obama gets a second term. But if he does, watch out.

And if you disagree with me then you, Sir, make Al Gore look smart.

Democratic Socialists believe that what's good for General Motors is good for the country.
Bankruptcy.

Daily Obama Jokes. 06/01/09

Michelle wanted diamonds for her birthday.
So Obama bought her a deck of cards.

Obama wants to control everything!
Get your protest permits now!

The Purpose Of The Supreme Court.

Well, we have a new justice nominated. Obama,
an attorney himself, praises her for empathy.
Huh?
What is the function of the Supremes?
It's not justice.
It's not fairness.
It's not determining financial judgments
It's not about social engineering.
It's not about playing God.
It's about one thing and one thing only.
Determining the constitutionality of the laws and
rules and actions of the government.
A proper judge makes rulings based on the
Constitution. Note that said judge may not agree
that a given decision is fair or just. The sole
question is one of constitutionality. Judges write
opinions on their votes and decisions. A Supreme
Court judge is perfectly free to point out a
deficiency that needs to be addressed and is
certainly free to advocate change both as a
citizen and from his/her strength of position as a
bully pulpit.
But decisions should be based solely on the
Constitution.
Empathy, compassion or emotions of any sort
should play no part in the process.

Special Note!
At last! The Fox Report on Saturday 05/30/09 did
a story on nuclear fusion at the National Ignition
Facility! Fusion is the clean, safe, low

104

environmental impact solution to our power needs. I'm no greenie, but it certainly makes sense, especially when compared to awkward, land intensive ideas like devastating the countryside with Obama Quixote's windmills or pumping zillions of gallons of water into the ground o drive out shale oil. THE MEDIA SHOULD BE ALL OVER THIS! The National Ignition Facility is one piece of government spending that is smart and that I can support. Perfect Fusion, export it and you'll soon forget Government Motors.

And if you disagree with me then you, Sir, are worse than Torquemada.

Socialist Democrats believe that it's okay to help one group of people by putting a gun to the head of another.

Daily Obama Jokes 06/02/09

Queen Pelosi has so much fan mail it keeps 10 aides busy.
Writing it.

What will Obama do next election about the promises to the far left he broke?
He'll double cross that bridge when he comes to it.

Yesterday I referenced the National Ignition Facility. This is a project designed to produce the first energy positive fusion reaction. Fusion has been possible in the lab, but at a net energy loss for a variety of reasons. This project, set to fire in 2010, will show fusion to be viable and the way of the future. The fuel, hydrogen, is readily available from water. One gallon of water would produce energy equal to 300 gallons of gasoline. No greenhouse gases. No danger of a China Syndrome meltdown. No Three Mile Accidents. Safe, clean, unlimited power.
The greenies have been advocating things like solar and wind power. His Obaminess wants to produce green jobs with such. Both would use a tremendous amount of land and resources with an inadequate return. Before these bad ideas have even gotten off the ground physics has rendered them the 21st century equivalent of buggy whips.
Greenies aren't telling you about this, of course. One was even on Fox Report denouncing the project as a waste of taxpayer money.
Balderdash! The reason you don't hear about it is that it doesn't fit the greenies bass ackward agenda to utilize technologically inferior energy sources and control society. This is out of their control and therefore of no interest. True greenies would embrace this as the ultimate solution to our energy needs.

The National Ignition Facility website is impressive. You can view it at https://lasers.llnl.gov/ Take the tour, then get on the horn and email it to all your friends. Get the word out that fusion is on the way and we need to get behind it.

And If you disagree with me then you, Sir, are worse than Fu Manchu.

Socialists Democrats think child molesters should get second chances and veterans are dangerous.

Daily Obama Jokes 06/03/09

What's Obama's new title?
Autocrat.

When it comes to giving some socialist democrats stop at nothing.

Laptops For Gitmo

Yep, we're giving laptop computers to the prisoners at Gitmo. 17 of them to be exact.
I'm curious. Why?
These are guys we don't want. No one else in the world wants them either.
Perhaps it's part of the stimulus package?
Supporting the computer industry?
I guess these guys need something to do, Sitting around the old "G", drink in hand watching "24" only goes so far. And as long as they have cable, why not DSL as well? Besides, it would give them a chance to catch up with their loved ones and all. Personally, I'm beginning to think we should bring them into the U.S. We could find them a nice halfway house. Fix it up with some lawn gnomes. I hear there's place next door to Queen Pelosi's is available….

And if you disagree with me, then you, Sir, are worse than the Wicked Witch Of The West.

Daily Obama Jokes 06/04/09

How many Hollywood liberals does it take to
screw in a light bulb?
None, Hollywood liberals screw in Jacuzzis.

Nothing succeeds like secession.

Touring The Middle East

Obama is off touring the middle east. Peace is on
the way. Yay.
Hmmm.
When he was running for office Obama
emphasized his Christianity. Perhaps he had to as
some were accusing him of being a Muslim. In
Turkey his speech there emphasized his life in
the Muslim world when young. Can't wait for the
Egyptian speech.

Obama. All things to all people. Or, at least,
saying all things to all people.

Factoids:

Ben Bernake today came out and told congress
today that continued runaway spending would
threaten our economy.

The German chancellor came out and condemned
our spending practices.

Word is the Brown government in England will fall
in a week or so for emptying the government
treasury.

Pravda recently ran an article blaming us for
becoming too Marxist and dumbing down our kids

so the government could pull their crap.

Barney Frank is drafting legislation for the government to back up California's debt. And every other state and local government's debt as well. Hey, Barney, see Bernanke's comment, okay?

Burglars are using people's tweets on Twitter to find people on vacation so they can rob their houses.

Obama said the government didn't want to run GM. GM has been talking about moving the corporate headquarters from Detroit. They got a call from the White House.

Hmmm.

I think the hand basket is starting to smolder.

And if you disagree with me, then you, Sir, are worse than Howard The Duck.

Daily Obama Jokes 06/05/09

Is Queen Pelosi spoiled?
No. That's her perfume.

Why did Michele plant Cheerios in the Whitehouse garden?
She thought they were donut seeds.

One Country?

Are we one country? I don't think so. Stop to consider. We have three groups of people. On the left we have those who think a government run welfare state is some Utopian paradise. On the right we have people who think you earn your own way. That the country should be a Meritocracy. In the middle we have people who don't care much one way or the other, who prefer to remain uninvolved. When those on the left have power the right feels raped. When those on the right are in power the people on the left feel shafted. There are two warring parties in one land, each wishing the other would go away.
We're three groups in one country. Shouldn't we really be three groups in three countries? I think we should divide up the country into three and let each go their own way.
The right would get the gulf states and then follow the west bank up the Mississippi and Ohio rivers to Canada, across to Montana and Alaska.
The left would get all the states west of there. The east would go to the "who cares?" crowd.
Three countries, three different philosophies. Each leaving the other alone and pursuing its own destiny.

111

Sounds better than the political machines we have to deal with today.

Daily Obama Jokes 06/06/09

We are all cut from the same genetic mold.
Queen Pelosi is just a little bit moldier.

Michelle attended a social event wearing a lovely
mink jacket. An animal rights supporter
approached her and demanded, "Do you know
how much an animal had to suffer for you to
wear that coat?"
"How dare you call Barack an anima!"

"What would Jesus Do?"
I hate it when a socialist democrat tries to use
that line. They try and claim a moral high ground
in their thefts by saying Jesus helped the poor
and the sick and that's what they are trying to do.
So they must be like Jesus and are doing a
morally good thing?
Balderdash.
At the essence of this nonsense is the usual
socialist belief that an end justifies the means.
Jesus faced down the Sanhedrin multiple times
and not once did he tell them to take money from
worshippers and give it to others. Not once did
he tell the Romans who tried him that they
should be off giving money, let alone someone
else's money, to the poor. Not once did he reach
into the pocket of one and steal their wealth and
give it to another.
Jesus assisted people one by one, on a personal
basis. He didn't try to heal the all sick. He healed
those who came to him. He never took from one
to aid from another.
Jesus exhorted people to do the right thing
voluntarily as individuals. Give to the poor, yes.
Give. Aid the sick, yes. Aid. He did not advocate
or create the creation of government agencies to
steal and redistribute wealth. He never denied
the rights of the wealthy to their wealth. He
criticized what they did with it.

113

When Jesus fed the multitude he did not take from one and give to another. Instead, fish and bread were voluntarily given to him. He gave of himself to make it grow and feed the thousands. When he healed the sick he gave of himself. When he raised the dead he gave of himself. Remember the tale of the poor woman who came to the temple and gave her last few coins? There were rich around who had given much in a showy egoistical manner. They laughed at her. What if Jesus do? He praised the woman for giving her all and chastised the men for giving from a false generosity, for their own social gain. He did not tell the woman to keep her money because she couldn't afford to give. He did not tell the men they should give more or less. He addressed the souls of the individuals and what their behavior regarding money meant.

He exhorted people to the right thing for the right reasons as individuals.

And this points out another danger of the socialist democrat agenda. By taking from one to give to another they undermine the spirit. When one merely has to write a check to government once a year and the government is the all giving god, then why should one lift a finger in charity? The government will handle There is no need to take a personal responsibility. The government will handle hand it. I can devote my time and energy to me. If there is something wrong the government will handle it. Rather than uplift the socialist democratic agenda undermines spirituality on both a personal and societal level. Perhaps that is the idea.

Yet in truth the end of poverty comes when the poor give, not take. It is in the act of giving, not in taking, that we are uplifted, On a spiritual as well as material level.

Jesus respected property rights. He did not violate them. He knew the center of what was best for people was what was in their inner life,

not in physicality of what they had or gave. He
was concerned with the welfare of the total
person, not monetary well being. He respected
the right to choose, though he criticized what
choices some made.
Contrary to what some on the far left
manipulatively claim, Jesus was not a socialist.
So when some socialist democrat claims he's
following in the footprints of Jesus tell him simply
that Jesus gave of himself. He never stole form
one to redistribute to another.

And if you disagree with me then you, Sir, are
worse than Judas Iscariot.

National Ignition Facility. Fusion power for the
future.
1

Daily Obama Jokes 06/07/09

Obama recently had his personal library defaced. Joe Biden connected all the dots.

What's the difference between congress and a vampire?
Vampires quit sucking at your throat at sunrise.

Socialism Fails

Socialism always fails, at least by our standards. It stresses sameness and hence embraces, at best, inefficiency. Equality of income is a false standard, oft used. Take from those who have, give to those who don't. The problem is that there is not an equality of talent, intelligence ambition, attitude, skills, wisdom or insight. To hold back our best by denying them the rewards of those things that allow them to get ahead is to create an artificially sterile environment in which nothing can grow. Motivation is crushed, save for those questing for power within the sociopolitical framework.
Socialists, in some breach of basic logic, think it's fair to give to those who have not by taking from those who earned at what is effectively gunpoint. How is that fair to those who have earned? Most who participate in our society either are earning now or have earned in the past and seek in retirement to enjoy the fruits of their labors. Explain to me how it is fair to give rewards to those who have not had the motivation to do for themselves.
To be sure there is a small portion of the society that will legitimately depend on the rest of us. The autistic, the physically impaired, those with certain psychiatric disorders. We as a society do indeed have a moral obligation to take care of our own in such circumstances. But not necessarily through government. Religious

organizations, charities, foundations for such things can be established and people would cheerfully give.

Consider now the rest of society. As we are now there are many tiers of services and products. These run from high end, expensive goods to those which meet basic needs. Manufacturers, retailers, service personnel all exist catering to the specific clientele using those products. Reduce the society to a socialistic quagmire and this disappears. There is a need only for one or two types of cars. Only one type of canned veggies is really needed in your store. Only one type of home computer need be built. We can all wear the same utilitarian garb. Luxury industries like jewelry, boats, and high fashion disappear. Jobs are lost. Factories close. Innovation dies. More people go on the dole. Education degenerates into serving a least common denominator. The children are dumbed down. A cycle forms that leads us degeneratively into a land of shadows. Shadows of what we could be, once were, of things gone.

In a free society we always have opportunity available Is it equal opportunity for all? Not yet and probably never fully will be. But it provides the greatest amount of opportunity and flexibility for the greatest number. It's certainly better than the alternative, which, in teaching to the low point and restraining excellence within an environment of societal stagnation actually destroys opportunity.

If you want a world where the most you can hope for is to eat, sleep, have sex and watch cable television, then socialism may be for you. If you think there is more to life then this lowest common denominator existence then you'll agree that socialism belongs on the discredited dung heap of unworkable philosophies.

Ultimately, in its rhetorical and false quest for some mythic fairness, socialism creates the unfairest society of all. The one that denies the individual the opportunity, used or unused, to reach their fullest level of accomplishment and being.

And if you disagree with me, then you, Sir, are worse than bobbing for French fries.

National Ignition Facility. Fusion power for the future.

Daily Obama Jokes 06/08/09

Where did Obama stay on his Middle East junket?
At a Bedouin breakfast

Why does Obama set aside two hours every
Sunday evening?
He likes to watch 60 Minutes.

Egyptian Speech

We delivered and polished, the teleprompter was
in fine form. The speech seemed like another
campaign speech tome, though I am not sure
what he's running for. All things to all people is
how it came off. Some how, though, he keeps
seeming to put a personal belief system ahead of
his country,
Iran is a good example. He argued that we have
no business deciding who has nuclear
weapons. This guy needs to reread his Koran.
I've read it the Iranian leadership is a bunch of
religious whackos. If they believe this book
literally, which they claim they to, it will be their
religious duty to start a war with the West. They
venerate dying in the process. And it's their
destiny to rule the world, by the way. There's' no
negotiating with that. And I do believe we have a
right and Obama a responsibility to insure they
don't get them. Jawboning isn't going to get the
job done.
Hey, isn't Obama an anti gun guy? So why the
casual attitude about nukes?
Obama also maintained that we would no longer
tell other countries how to run their business. He
promptly told the Palestinians what they should
be doing, the Israelis what they should be doing
and the Muslim world how to treat women.
Our Lordship speaks in mysterious ways, his
blunders to perform.

119

Daily Obama Jokes 06/09/09

Daily Obama Jokes

A liberal running for his first public office, boldly proclaimed, "I've kept regular hours for over ten years!"
"Oh?" asked a reporter. "What were you in for?"

Do I think Obama's a fool?
No, but what is my opinion against millions of others?

Hats off to Justice Ruth Bader Ginsburg. The Obama machine has been running roughshod over the legal system to get the Chrysler bankruptcy through on his Obaminess's terms. Some bondholders, trying to get heard, filed an emergency appeal to the Supreme Court to slow things down and get a hearing. Judge Ginsburg, empowered to hear the appeal, granted the bondholders their due and suspended the process until they could get a court review.
How will Chrysler's takeover/bankruptcy end up? Not well, we wager. Buy it was nice to see Ginsburg, a liberal, wasn't just following in line. This decision shows integrity and in a spirit of fairness we must give Justice Ginsburg the tip of our hat.

And if you disagree with me, then you, sir, are worse than tofu.

National Ignition Project. Fusion power for our future.

Daily Obama Jokes 06/10/09

What shape is the world?
Watching the Dems it's not round. It's not flat.
It's crooked.

What will His Obaminess never say in an after
dinner speech?
"Give me the check."

I originally published today's blog entry on
associated content with rights retained.

Let's look at what the socialist democrats in
Washington have done. They've bought into 80%
of AIG, Turned General Motors into Government
Motors with majority stake at a cost that may
run as high as $70 billion. More billions on a 20%
stake of Chrysler. Loser companies all. Bailed out
the banking system, while effectively
commandeering a certain amount of control over
at least some of the institutions, with a nearly
$800 billion dollar check. Put in a dubious
stimulus $800 billion package that's 90% social
programs.
"Only government is big enough," blared His
Obaminess on clips aired repeatedly on CNN, Fox
News, MSNBC and else where.
Oh, give me a break......Hey, that's exactly what
he should do
We need a national bail out the little guy day. As
long as all these trillions are being spent by the
powerful for the powerful, why not toss some to
the little guy? The taxpayer. The voter. I think
His Obaminess would be wise to pay off the
credit card bills of all Americans. Simply get a
settlement figure from the various credit card
issuers, print up some more of those magic
money from nothing dollar bills and cut them a
check.
Think of the benefits. With all credit card debt

gone many people having problems paying their mortgages would have the cash flow to keep their homes. No tons of paperwork and refinancing and such needed. The Christmas season would be an economic miracle as consumers would now have the cash flow to buy presents galore. Auto sales would be saved. Government Motors would be saved. Debt collectors would be tossed out of work. His Obaminess could buy more votes than ever before! The list is endless.

Let's start a movement now to get His Obaminess to really help out the little guy instead of playing Monopoly with our money and the boys on Wall Street. In October we make photocopies of all our credit card bills. We blank out all account info. It's not needed by some smart aleck aide in the mail room. We draft a little note: "Dear Sire, Enclosed are my credit card bills. Please bail me out. Sincerely yours, " etc. On November first we all mail them in.

Why November first? Well, to give the idea time to circulate and grow. Tea parties weren't built in a day, you know.

The White House Mailing Address is:

The White House
1600 Pennsylvania Ave. NW
Washington D.C., 20502

Spread the word Let's get a movement going and inundate the White House with our bills. Let's get a bailout for "We The People!"

And if you disagree with me than you, Sir, are worse than Arlen Specter.

National Ignition Facility. Fusion power for the future.

Daily Obama Jokes 06/11/09

Obama is the Mae 'West president.
His motto? "I done 'em wrong."

The UAW is striking for shorter hours. 60
minutes is just too long.

Why independents and liberals need to watch Fox
News

Factoid: An Ohio State University study recently
showed that conservatives. are more open to
counter arguments than liberals..
Hmmm.
Who is it who tells you what to listen to and what
not? Who is it who denigrates and ridicules
opposition views and depends on that ridicule
more then any thing else? Even his Obaminess
has used his office as a bully pulpit to make
untrue allegations about news facilities that
openly oppose his wants. Only one side in the
political debate tries to control your mind.
If you are an independent or even a liberal you
need to listen to the other side. For your own
freedom of choice. To not just follow suit as the
medias elite tells you what not to do. You need
to be a "bad boy." To learn that the pablum
spouted by the media elite is little more than
drool spooned out to keep you in their fold.
Take a week. Judge not. Watch Fox news. Spend
a week listening to Glenn Beck. Tivo him if the
time he's on is inconvenient. Fox News Watch,
airing several times over the weekend, is
excellent commentary on media behavior.
Hannity (whom I find personally grating) and
O'Reilly may prove too bombastic for some. So
watch On The Record with the always civil Greta
Van Susteren. The Fox news business block airs
Saturday morning from 10 A.M to noon . Charles

Payne is a personal favorite amongst the regulars. There are also worthy counterpoint programs on CNBC. Tune in the Kudlow Report at 7 PM and CNBC reports with Dennis Kneale at 8pm.

If you are a liberal or independent you need to watch these shows. Not to be converted. To be aware. To be informed. For yourself so you may be secure in the knowledge that you are your own person, not an elite media created sheeple. Compare these shows with the liberal pundits on the leftist MSNBC. Decide for yourself who is hate filled. After being informed.

I was a liberal once in the days of my youth. I got tired of the lies, deceptions, and manipulations.

Don't be as I was. Open yourself up to more and actually listen to other sides.

And if you disagree with me then you, Sir, are worse than a tuna smoothie.

Daily Obama Jokes 06/12/09

"Where is Washington?"
"He's dead."
"No, I mean the capital of the United States."
"Invested in bankrupt companies."

A soldier returned home from Iraq and was
catching up on local politics.
"We've got a new democratic
congressman," informed his wife.
"What's he like?"
"Whiskey... gin... fast women..."

Good Guys Down The Drain

The 06/11/09 Cleveland Plain Dealer had an
interesting article concerning car dealers. Seems
that virtually all of them in the area support local
community causes and charities. From things like
uniforms for
 kid's sport teams to cars for charity church
raffles. One Kia dealer awards a new car every
year to one graduating student of a certain high
school each year. It's a big student event. All the
kids who meet certain requirements for
attendance and grades are given a car key and
one by one they try the key in the door of the
giveaway car. The kid with the lucky key gets the
car. Seems this motivates borderline kids to
work harder, to get into the drawing.
So what's the point?
Hmmm.
The Obama plan is forcing thousands of
dealerships to close. That's thousands of
communities that will be left without a valuable
supportive resource. Thousands of communities
less well positioned to self assist. Thousands of
communities that will be less independent. And
when you re less dependent on yourself you are
more dependent on......

Color me paranoid but his Obaminess's ideas never seem to promote self dependence. They always seem to promote dependence on government. His government. Even if the effect is unintended.

And if you disagree with me than you, Sir, are worse than pork tartare.

Daily Obama Jokes 06/13/09

Why are Obama's ideas so hard to grasp?
Manure is slippery when wet.

How can congress regulate the economy when
they can't practice any?

Mini Nukes

Babcox and Wilcox has a new, small nuclear
reactor, the mReactor. Each 125 megawatt
reactor would be able to produce enough power
for a city of 100,000. The new reactor would
have its components and assembly done in
factories in the U. S. Read "Jobs"
people. Residential and commercial applications
abound.
Whoops! One small problem.
The Nuclear Regulatory Commission has no plans
to even review the plans until 2011. No money
for people to do so says the NRC.
Hmmm.
Isn't Obama the green president?
So why is it we have a bailout bill with 90% of
the 800 million going to social programs? Why do
we have billions to "invest" in the likes of AIG
and Government Motors? We can't fund Medicare
and Social Security but have money for a
national health care program? .Why is it we think
it's a good idea to fight Global Moaning with an
expensive carbon tax?
Yet when a good idea, new technology, comes
along it can't even get reviewed?
We've got Don Quixote in the White House
chasing windmills while worthy ideas lie wasting
on the barren land of 'Washington. This guy is
no savior, just a pedantic demagogue filled with
preconceived notions of how the world should be
and an unrelentingly arrogant drive to bring that
misshapen vision about.

And if you disagree with me then you, Sir, are worse than week old sushi.

National Ignition Facility. Fusion power for our future

Daily Obama Jokes 06/14/09

What do Chicago and Iran have in common?
It's not who votes that matters, it's who counts
the votes.

I wish Obama would speak his mind. His
speeches would be so much shorter.

Bail Out The Little Guy Redux

We suggested a few days ago that Obama bail
out the little guy by paying off credit card
debt. A blurb on the news today said that
Americans owed 2.5 trillion excluding their
mortgages. No mention was made of autos. Let's
assume its all credit cards.
Bush spent 800 billion bailing out banks.
Obama's spending 800 million on new social
programs, excuse, me stimulus, add in an
estimated 90 billion final cost for Chrysler and
Government Motors nationalization and another
trillion for new health care. That's about 2.7
trillion.
Obama keeps claming he's saving jobs, an
impossible to prove or quantify assertion. If his
Obaminess wants to save the people he could
start simply by paying off the people's debts. It
would do more to stimulate us than what he's
doing to us now.

And if you disagree with me, then you ,Sir, are
worse than a horny pit bull humping my leg.
.
National Ignition Facility. Fusion power for the
future.
1

Daily Obama Jokes 06/15/09

Have you tried the new dance, the Obama Shuffle?
Two steps forward, one step back and sidestep..

Obmanomics
Shortages shall be equally distributed amongst the people

Pain for, er, Paying For Health Care

Let's see if we can add this up. Obama says you won't have to sign up for his socialist health care program. From elsewhere in this socialist democratic autocracy we hear that health care benefits will be taxed as income.
So if you don't sign up for the National Socialist health care plan you get punished with extra taxes. The government will make you feel pain for not participating in their dictatorial plan.
Gee, thanks guys.
Remember that campaign promise where people making less than $250k wouldn't get
taxed? How many of you have private health insurance and make less then 250k? The vast majority, I'm sure. And you'll be taxed if you don't knuckle under.
What's more if health care benefits get taxed as income there will be a number of you reading who will find yourself bumped into a higher bracket.
Don Quixote is not only chasing windmills, he's throwing you into the whirling blades.

And if you disagree with me then you, Sir, are worse than potato salad that's sat in the sun all day.

National Ignition Facility. Fusion power for the future.

Daily Obama Jokes 06/16/09

A young guy applied to volunteer for the Democrat's campaign.
"Well," asked the local campaign manager, "do you ever tell lies?"
"No, sir, but I can learn."

The dollar really goes far these days. I can go weeks without finding something one will buy."

It Ain't The Rich

Have you ever noticed how many rich Democrats support tax increases on the wealthy? It's not because they are self sacrificing or patriotic or good hearted. It's because it's to their power and wealth advantage.
Let's go back to 2004. Kerry vs. Bush with Kerry wanting to raise taxes. Tax returns were disclosed. The Bush family paid taxes at a 28% rate on an income of about $800k. The Kerry's paid taxes at an 18% rate on an income of $5 million.
Yep, the Kerry family made 6 times what the Bush family did and paid taxes at a 10% lower rate. How did that happen?
The Kerrys, as it turns out, were heavily invested in triple tax free municipal bonds. These bonds pay interest free of local, state and federal taxes. The higher the tax rate the better this investment is. For the wealthy. Make no mistake, the Kerrys did nothing immoral, illegal or fattening. They simply took advantage of the tax law. It's perfectly legal for the rich and poor alike to do so. It's just that it takes cash, and lots of it, to make the strategy really effective. Too bad the poor don't have the cash.
There are many other little things the rich can do to increase their wealth while taxes are avoided. One can buy a stock and hold it for an extended

131

term, for example. As the stock appreciates in value the wealthy get wealthier and yet pay no taxes. There is no tax due without a sale of the stock and a taxable gain. If the wealthy person dies the stock goes to an heir. There is then a new tax basis for the stock, the closing price of the stock on the day of death of the original owner. The stock can now be sold for virtually no gain whatsoever. And so wealth passes between the generations free of the tax man.

These types of wealth preservation and accumulation are available to the rich and poor alike. It's just that they are only useful to the who have already.

The rich Dems don't mind the tax increases. They will legally avoid most of it. So who are the real targets?

What are these tax hikes about?

As we shall see tomorrow, it's not about fairness.

And if you disagree with me, then you, Sir, are worse than the Dred Scott decision.

National Ignition Facility. Fusion power for the future.

Daily Obama Jokes 06/17/09

What is Charlie Rangel's favorite work of fiction?
His income tax return.

Queen Pelosi was walking along the Potomac. A
man in the river floundering cried out, "Help me!
Help me! I can't swim!"
"So?" replied the queen. "I can't play piano, but
you don't hear me complaining about it."

Soaking HENRY

First I would like to acknowledge that the concept
of the HENRY comes from the book "The
Millionaire Mind" by Dr. Thomas J. Stanley. It's a
most worthwhile book and several concepts in
today's blog are thanks to him.
Yesterday I showed that the rich can avoid the
brunt of a tax the rich strategy. So who is it that
does get taxed?
Before going further let us differentiate between
wealth and income. Wealth, quite simply, is what
you have. Income is what you take in, i.e.: earn.
They are two different and distinct things. All the
tax proposals for soaking the rich are geared for
taxing income. The truly rich can sidestep this.
So who gets taxed? The HENRYs of the world.

High
Earning
Not
Rich
Yet

Doctors. lawyers, executives,
entrepreneurs, small businessmen and more
become the targets in the tax the rich shell game.
These are often people with substantial incomes

133

who have not accumulated the asset base to truly be classified as wealthy. Quite often these people do have nice houses, cars, kids in private schools, etc. The substantial income is used to provide a better class lifestyle for their families. Wealth, the possession of permanent assets that can grow in value, is not held in abundance. But asset investments are usually being made to get there. Others in this category are small businessmen sinking their earnings back into their business, looking to grow into wealth that way, They aren't there yet.

The end result is that the first victims of the tax the rich fallacy are the upper middle class. The rich continue to maintain and advance their wealth while those just below them are beaten down by the onerous tax burden. The "substantial" income becomes worth less both in real terms and in terms of purchasing power (taxes are inflationary, something rarely mentioned). The HENRYs are forced to cut back in their lifestyle. The reduced spending ripples down through the economy, causing the beginnings of a downward economic spiral. More importantly, from the standpoint of the taxed, it impedes the ability of HENRYs to accumulate assets in the quest for actual wealth.

The rich dodge the tax bullet. The HENRYs are the first hammered. The goal of wealth becomes progressively harder to attain. The gap between the wealthy and other classes, something socialist democrats complain about, continues to widen.

And rich democrats keep their money and power while eliminating threats from below.

And if you disagree with me then you, Sir, are worse than Rasputin

National Ignition Facility. Fusion power for the future.

Daily Obama Jokes 06/18/09

Is there free speech in Iran?
Sure. You can talk your head off.

When Queen Pelosi got married who was the
lucky man?
Her father.

The Tax The Rich Downward Spiral.

Let's recap the last couple days
Wealth is what you have. Income is what you
make. Having income is not the same as being
rich.
The rich are quite able to sidestep tax the rich
schemes.
The real people punished by tax the rich schemes
are the HENRYs.

High Earning Not Rich Yet.

The HENRYs are the strongest force building the
economy. Hammer them and they have less to
invest America. Jobs, productivity and economic
activity are damaged. As a result the HENRYs end
up earning less. The windfall from the first year
or two of tax the rich drops. Meanwhile the
government needs (read "wants") more money.
The definition of rich currently is supposed to be
an income of $250k. Of, course income does not
equate to wealth, but that doesn't matter. The
target has been drawn. The $250k number is
arbitrary. So the number gets changed
downward. Say 200k. And the process starts all
over again. And again.
Meanwhile there is a 50% portion of the
population not paying any taxes. Many get
checks consisting of other people's money. The
socialist democrats can't tax them. They are a
potential source of class warfare votes. The 45%

between the poor and the rich take the brunt of the beating.

So the government taxes productivity, thus actually lowering its tax stream across time. Then it comes up with more tricks. Carbon taxes, Vat taxes, etc. These hurt everybody, even lower income people. Perhaps some more wealth redistribution (actually the impoverishment of society) comes into play to cling to the poor vote by covering these additional regressive taxes. The end result is that we have a society in which upward mobility and the attainment of wealth becomes difficult and perhaps virtually impossible. Instead we have a forced downward mobility of all but the wealthiest classes. We replace progress with regress and spiral into a morass in which mere survival, mere "getting along" replaces the drive to achieve greatness.

And if you disagree with me then you, Sir, are worse than a hemlock nightcap.

Daily Obama Jokes 06/19/09

Can Reverend Wright heal the sick?
His every sermon cures insomnia

Why do UAW workers hate vacations?
They have to drink coffee on their own time.

Today's blog entry has been previously published on Associated Content with rights retained.

Barack Obama needs to go on Fox News.
Tuesday in an interview on CNBC Obama again complained about Fox News not liking him. This is far from the first time. Fox had a field day on Wednesday playing various clips of Obama expressing his displeasure over Fox. "They don't like me." he complained.
Obama seems very concerned about being liked. He seems to be confusing his policies with his personhood. If you don't like his policies you must not like him. It strikes me as rather narcissistic .
The end result though is that Obama keeps appearing in favorable venues fielding softball questions. Showing up on shows where he can dominate the conversation and do most of the talking. Most of the media outlets still seem to be having a love affair with this guy. Only Fox seems to be willing to challenge him regularly. And that is exactly why he needs to do interviews on Fox News.
There are plenty of hard questions to be asked of Obama and his administration's policies and decisions. Why was $20 billion sunk into GM to keep it out of bankruptcy followed by more billions committed along with a government ownership stake secured in a subsequent bankruptcy? Same with Chrysler. Why was the UAW put ahead of senior bond holders in the bankruptcies, despite the law being to the

contrary? Why are we apologizing to the world in tour after tour across the international landscape? Why are prisoners from Gitmo being released into tropical paradises, accompanied by what amount to bribes to the local government? Should the government really be taking a 34% interest in Citigroup? Why is his stimulus package 90% social programs and why is it most of the package doesn't go into effect until 2010, an election year, when the economy is struggling now? Are his policies not a simplistic and apparent attempt to move the country into being a socialist state? And I haven't even started on questions about healthcare, Israel and Iran..

The softball venues ask simplistic questions and smile and nod at the answers. Fox News doesn't and they have the largest viewer ship amongst the news channels. Obama truly believes in his paradigms, that they are correct. The way to prove this is to meet his doubters and detractors head on. Socrates never ducked an argument. It seems Obama is no Socrates. If Obama really wants to convince people he needs to take on the opposition head on and prove it.

It's cowardly to appear on CNBC and deny Fox's lead business news analyst, Neil Cavuto, an audience, er, interview. During the campaign Obama did an interview with Bill O'Reilly. O'Reilly neither bit his head off nor rolled over. It was quite fair. I can understand a reluctance to not talk with the always bombastic Sean Hannity, but there is no excuse for not interviewing with the always congenial Chris Wallace. Even mild mannered Greta Van Susteren, who has issued an open invitation to Obama, would be a good start. I can't think of a reason not to talk with her.

Ducking Fox News is cowardly. He needs to meet his critics face to face. Until he does there will be ongoing doubts not only about the quality of his decisions and policies but also his courage and integrity.

Barack Obama needs to go on Fox News. Whether or not he can withstand the scrutiny is a question important only to him. Either way the American public would win.

Daily Obama Jokes 06/20/09

There's a new disease afflicting the socialist democrats.
Spendicitis.

Obama's Dictionary: Dime
What's left of a dollar when he's done with it.

Prime Time Spam

The assault from the left wing media continues. ABC will be bootlicking His Obaminess with a one hour special from the White House on Obamacare. A one hour unopposed socialist infomercial.

There will be no equal time.
There will be no opposing view.
There will be no hard questions.

I fear the end is near for us when the media not only gives tacit approval to socialism but begins to actively act in collusion with the administration to bring it about. The National Socialist propaganda mill is rapidly being constructed, it seems.

And if you disagree with me then you, Sir, are worse than ABC.

National Ignition Facility. Fusion power for the future.

Daily Obama Jokes 06/21/09

Patriots think every day is July 4th.
Obama thinks every day is April 15th.

Liberalism.
The haunting, scared feeling that someone
somewhere can take care of themselves without
government assistance.

Iran: The Sound Of Silence

The White House has been pretty silent on the
Iranian quasi-revolution to date. The Senate and
House have been issuing proclamations, of
course, but Obama has been holding off. For this
many have been criticizing him.
Sorry, but for once I'm in his camp on this one.
Never try to catch a cat in the middle of fight.
Notice, if you will, that several days after the
protests started the Iranian leadership tried to
claim interference from the U.S was to blame.
Sorry, but there's nowhere to hang that hat. The
Iranian leaders were striving to try and find a
common enemy to turn attention to. A tactic
they've employed before. By keeping out of the
mix Obama has denied the Iranian leadership of
a favorite tactic.
Make no mistake, the time will come when a
louder voice will be called for, but I don't think it
is yet. So let the Congress do the squealing. They
aren't the focus of the world's attention, Obama
is. And so far refusing to play has been the right
decision. Which only goes to show even a blind
hog finds an acorn once in a while.

And if you disagree with me, then you, Sir, are
worse than a double chili cheeseburger before
bedtime.

Daily Obama Jokes 06/22/09

What was the real problem with Iranian election? Clerical errors.

John Kerry and a buddy were out hunting when a beautiful babe appeared out of the brush. "Wow," whispered Kerry's buddy, "she looks good enough to eat!"
So Kerry shot her.

Health Care Fairy Tale

Okay, enough being nice to Obama. Did you catch his speech at the medical convention? What a pack of horse hooey. Obama claimed, with a straight face, that he wanted a national health system to compete with private insurance, not replace it. Soooo…. You get to be the referee, the rule maker, and have a team in the game. Sound like a fair sport to you? Didn't think so. Obama also claimed that competition with a public health program would force private insurance to improve. Competition is good, right? The problem with this rationalization is that there are, according to a news report I saw Sunday, 1300 health insurers in this country already. Sounds like there is plenty of competition to me. Then he actually said there are plenty of countries with national health plans the citizenry were happy with. In a subsequent press briefing his press secretary couldn't name a single one.
The fact is that the Obama plan is an ideal opening gambit for attacking privatized health care. An eventual Obamacare system would supplant it. The media has raised in uproar (curiously, only when Bush was in office, Hmm…) about 5,000 American deaths in Iraq. A national health plan would probably kill tens of thousands each year via neglect and rationing. And the media would be complicit.

Obama's proposals?
As the legendary Nero Wolfe would say,
"Flummery!"

And if you disagree with me, then you , Sir, are
worse than a butt burp.

National Ignition Facility. Fusion power for the
future.

Daily Obama Jokes 06/23/09

Government waste costs billions but at least we're getting plenty for our money.

Under Obama the only thing we'll be able to get with a quarter is heads or tails.

The Jobs Report

Steve Jobs, the leader of Apple Computer, returned to work yesterday, Seems he had a liver transplant. Steve Jobs is worth megabucks, undoubtedly covered by insurance that will pay most of his costs, He's earned his position by being an exceedingly productive member of society.
What about the homeless person who needs a liver transplant? What does he do? Dies, most likely. Democratic socialists would tell you that this unfair. The homeless person is a human being too and has just as much right to live as Steve Jobs. And that society should insure this right by paying for the transplant.
Actually this situation sounds more like natural selection to me. The more advanced member of the species gets to survive. Science.
Now I might sound heartless in saying this, but I'm not. I'm just being dispassionate in how I look at this. If I had the power of a Jesus I would gladly cure both.
But I have to ask what would happen in a nationalized system. Would both men get liver transplants? What would the cost be? What happens if there were a shortage of livers? Would we have a lottery? Would Steve Jobs and the homeless man have an equal chance to live or die? How would that work exactly?
In every nationalized system I've ever heard of scarce resources get rationed, Especially for the elderly. You are evaluated for productivity and

potential contribution to society. When you stop being productive resources stop being allocated to you. You are allowed to die while someone younger, stronger, more productive gets to live. The "you're human too and deserve the treatment" argument flies out the
window, Because resources, livers n this case, are limited. The resource need not be livers, incidentally. It could be operating rooms available, surgeon availability, money, what have you. It doesn't matter. The productive one gets the resource.
So, again, the superior member of the species gets to survive.
The profit motive gives reason to expand resources. Where there is money to be made creative people will find more ways to deliver services and meet needs. Take out the profit motive, nationalize health care, and there is no reason to expand resources. Not only does the homeless guy buy the farm, more people get denied treatment because the resources aren't there.
So I say keep government out of the health care business and let the creative folk work their magic. That is how more treatment will get to more people in the long run.
And to any arguments to the contrary I say "Pfui"

And if you disagree with me then you, Sir, are worse than Dr. Strangelove.

National Ignition Facility. Fusion power for the future.

Daily Obama Jokes 06/24/09

How many socialist democrats does it take to
change a light bulb?
Here, Comrade, use this candle.

Obamanomics
Change you can smell.

The Bank Response

Citigroup has announced this morning, according
to CNBC, that it will be raising salaries, some as
much as 50%, and issuing new stock options to
try and retain employees. This due to the bonus
system being seriously curtailed.
True enough, the bonus system got abused by
some, but it was integral to talent retention, Ever
wonder how it got started? The U.S. Congress.
Back in 1995 congress, in an attempt to raise
revenues, made salaries and commissions in
excess of one million dollars non tax deductible
to the corporation. Bonuses were not included in
this. So companies did the obvious thing,
reducing salaries and commissions and instituting
bonus programs. In point of fact many of the
people who earned and received bonuses that
were much maligned and strong armed back
would have received commissions instead under
the old system. Only the most fanatical socialist
would deny a sales person their commission. But
call it a bonus and they become a target....

So congress was responsible for:

An abusable bonus system
Bad bank loans forced by legislation
Failure to oversee Fannie and Freddie Mac
The dismantling of banking system safe guards
that has worked since the 1930's

The SEC was responsible for:
Failure to enforce rules that prevented bear raids
on stock.
Approval of and failure to regulate mortgage
backed securities and credit default swaps.

The Fed:
Was responsible for an overly loose monetary
policy.

They are from the government and they're here
to help us. And it's capitalism that's failed?

I don't think so.

And if you disagree with me, then you Sir, are
worse than an attack by rabid squirrels.

Daily Obama Jokes 06/25/09

Capital punishment means never having to say "You again!"

Capital Punishment
Obama's taxing and spending policies.

Issa vs. Bernanke

Today is the big shootout on the hill. Issa vs. Bernanke. First let me mention to the media that it is Issa with a long "I". I've been irritated by news guys calling him "EEssa." Cramer did it all through a rant last night. I knew Darrell in high School. We were on the stage crew together and, unless he's changed it, it's a long "I."
It's a simple 4 letter name, so get it right guys.
So what's this about? A cover up? Superficially.
If you recall the Davis recall in California Issa led the charge then, too, I thought it was pretty obvious that Issa not only wanted to hang Davis but that he wanted the governorship for himself. Enter ARNIE. Ooops. So much for that idea.
Thus Darrell retreated back into the shadows, popping up every once in a while to give a conservative perspective on things.
Now there is a power vacuum in the Republican party. Governors who can't keep it in their pants. Ex governors standing up and saying, "I'm the conservative!" The last candidate for president was a quasi-liberal who shot himself in the foot repeatedly.
Opportunity.
Enter Issa the gunslinger, taking aim at Ben Bernanke. Looking to make his bones ala Elliot Spitzer. It's about power, in my opinion,. Aiming for the senatorial seat perhaps. Perhaps more.
Like I said, I knew Darrell in high school. He wanted liked. Respected. To be a leader. He

148

failed.

I think he has those same needs now and I don't really think it's about Bernanke. It doesn't mean he's wrong (or right, for that matter), only that there is more at play here.

And if you disagree with me, then you, Sir, are worse than cold French fries.

National Ignition Facility. Fusion power for the future.

Daily Obama Jokes 06/26/09

What business does Obama really want to be in?
Yours.

Obama wants to follow in the footsteps
of Herbert Hoover. He was the first president to give his salary back. Now he wants everybody to do it.

Did anyone notice the Chinese bought a Canadian oil company this week? The Chinese have been buying hard assets and raw materials throughout the world. Every where but here. So has Russia. They have long term contracts with Libya and others and have even tried to stake out the North Pole.
His Obaminess? Wealth through takeover of failed corporations? Prosperity through higher taxes? Nirvana via social programs? Power by endless acres of windmills and solar panels? The bliss of cap and trade? Happiness is being turned into a government wage slave to pay for endless spending we don't need?
Blessings through government rationed healthcare?
I think His Obaminess has this vision where we all work eight hours for the state, go home and watch cable tv.
I have a vision where we beat the Europeans to fusion power (they have a fusion plant, Project Iter, set to fire 2016).
I have a vision where we actually teach our kids to do stuff, where we teach them to learn how to learn, to innovate and move ahead. Not an education system geared to turning them into homogenized drones of the social order.
I have a vision where we reach for the stars, not sit on our butts while the Russians plan lunar expeditions.

I have a vision where the country provides equal opportunity for all, not where those who can do have it ripped away and dispersed to those who can't
I have a vision of a country where the spirit and power of personal charity supports a true brotherhood, not a soul stifling morass of government hold up programs that disincentivizes all.
I have a vision where families take care of each other, not get torn apart by government care giving.
What we dream and what we need to dream of will never happen under Obama.
Kumbaya.

And if you disagree with me them you, Sir, are worse than a sharp stick in the eye.

National Ignition Facility. Fusion power for the future.

Daily Obama Jokes 06/27/09

Why is Obama luckier at cards than at the horses?
They don't let him shuffle the horses.

My local bookstore now has references on making
money listed under "Fiction."

Crap And Trade

Yep, that's what it is.
This totally unnecessary tax will hurt everybody.
It is totally regressive. Those that least afford it
will have a heavy burden to bear. It's also a
betrayal of His Obaminess's promise not to raise
taxes on people making $250k or less.
Not that that surprises anybody with a lick of
sense. Hey, liberals. He's taking it out of your
pocket, too,
Things couldn't get worse, right?
Prediction.
If this goes into law the socialist democrats will
realize that the poor won't be able to pay for this
boondoggle. So of course they will have to help
them. And how will they do that? By reaching
more deeply into the pockets of those they call
"rich," That means lowering the definition of rich
again and raising rates of some type.
And since the definition of rich is skewed, based
on income and not wealth, the ones that will
really get hammered are the HENRYs.

High
Earning
Not
Rich
Yet.

Doctor? That means you.
Lawyer? That means you.
Executive? That means you.

152

Small business man? That means you.
Investor? That means you.
Entrepreneur? That means you.

Get the picture.
I greatly fear crap and trade is just the start
of the nightmare, not the end.

And if you disagree with me then you, Sir, are
worse than 8 republican turncoats.

National Ignition Facility. Fusion power for the
future.

Daily Obama Jokes 06/28/09

I wouldn't mind Queen Pelosi taking military transport if she'd only go where I want her to...

His Obaminess wants a new national anthem. Czars And Stripes

Hot Dog

I initially gave His Obaminess a pass for holding his forked tongue on the Iranian election. Once they started accusing us of interfering he was free to do more. So he did minimal whimpering. Saw him live in Germany as he said the Iranians really should think about what they are doing. Pathetic.
I guess our Community Organizer In Chief isn't quite up to organizing the world community.
In the meantime a previous invitation to Iranian diplomats to attend 4th of July celebrations at our embassies across the world stands.
"Tsk. Tsk. .Naughty. Naughty. Here have a hotdog."
And Obama becomes Caterer in Chief.

Oh, by the way don't hesitate to remind liberals Iran has gun control.

And if you disagree with me, then you, Sir, are worse than "Plan 9 From Outer Space."

National Ignition Facility. Fusion power for the future."

Daily Obama Jokes 06/29/09

Who's the greatest pirate of all time?
Cap'n Trade

America is the land of opportunity.
We all have the opportunity to work for the
government. As taxpayers.

So Now What?

Okay, Obama has done nothing in Iran. Can't get
involved and all that.
So now what about Honduras? The military just
tossed out the duly elected socialist president
hours before he could get power grabbing
legislation passed. Yep, he was elected. Yep, he
was betraying his people. Yep, the military tossed
him out.
Every one on the continent, the Useless Nations,
Obama and Hillary are "concerned" and
democracy should be followed.
But what do you do when the guy you elected
betrays you? When the only action available in
the time line is outside the law?
Seems to me you rebel.
Democracy needs trust. Trust requires honesty.
Dishonesty has already invalidated the system.
So now what I think the Hondurans, if everyone
buts out, would be fine. But Hugo Chavez is
threatening military action.
If he goes down that road what will his
Obaminess do? Express more concern With all
the concern he's expressing he's more worried
that a hypochondriac in a quarantine ward.
Or will ha act? Will he keep Chavez out of
Honduran affairs as he has kept us out of Iranian
affairs? Will he meet force with force
He should.
Or will he, shudder, stand aside, or, worse yet,
tacitly approve such an action?

North Korea. Iran
Failure.
Now Honduras. Our own hemisphere.
Our rights were violated. We fought. The
Hondurans' rights were about to be violated.
They fought. I hope Obama gets, it. But my
guess is….

And if you disagree with me than you, Sir, are
worse than a Chicago politician.

National Ignition Facility. Fusion power for the
future.

Daily Obama Jokes 06/30/09

Why was God able to create the world in only 6 days?
No unions.

Remember when judges suspended the bad guys instead of the sentences?

California, Here We Come....

Today His Obaminess was on T.V hyping his job destruction, er, Cap And Trade bill. He was citing California as a shining example of energy efficiency.
Later on CNBC, in an unrelated story, they were giving some facts on California.
It's up to its eyeballs on unsustainable debt it can't pay.
Kind of like the Federal government.
It's got sky high taxes
Kind of like Obama is proposing on income, health care and energy.
California ranked 50th of 50 states in business climate. Since 2001 30% of manufacturing jobs have exited the state.
Kind of like companies will move even more jobs overseas if Obama gets his onerous and self serving tax plans passed.
California is a shining example, all right.
From Gold Rush to bum rush.

And if you disagree with me then you, Sir, are worse than taxation with representation.

National Ignition Facility. Fusion power for the future.

Daily Obama Jokes 07/01/09

Obama stands on his record.
That way we can't see it.

Barack Obama
Putting the U.S.A. under a pedestal.

High Cost Of Ed

Last week Cramer went on that prices were falling throughout the country. Except in two areas. Health care and education.
What do these two things have in common? Third party payers. Third party payers always drive up costs because the provider of a good or service has no reason to look to your bottom line.
Let's take universities for example. Every university has a financial aid department. Their job is to find you money to turn over to the school. Grants, scholarships and, especially, student loans. The latter is the worst part. You get shopped around for money and end up in debt to get this wonderful education. There is no attempt to reduce costs. You never see universities pitch themselves on affordability. You are simply a check to be brought in. There is no need to keep an eye on their expenses or your costs because a third party fronts the money and you pay it back later.
What's worse, they'll get you in any major you want. But what if that liberal arts degree sticks you in a field that isn't well paid? Now you're stuck with the loan and a useless degree and four years wasted.
Let me tell you a true story.
A couple years back I was shopping for a car. The sales lady and I chatted as we drove around on some test drives. Seems she was a theater major in college. I asked what she was doing selling cars. She replied she couldn't get a job in theater

that pays enough to allow her to pay back her student loan.

So, fueled by the third party student loan racket university costs keep spiraling upward. It's as bad as the credit card rip-offs. At least those guys have to put everything in small print.

And if you disagree with me than you, Sir, are worse than a C in art appreciation.

National Ignition Facility. Fusion power for the future.

Daily Obama Jokes 07/02/09

All Joke Day!

Why did Michelle marry Obama?
She likes the simple things in life!

The income we used to dream of we can't live on today.

Unions are now demanding unskilled labor get more than skilled labor because it's harder for unskilled labor to do the work.

What's the difference between a grape and a liberal?
You take off your shoes to stomp in a grape.

How many liberals does it take to change a light bulb?
Only one, but a conservative has to show him how.

What's the difference between an anchor and a liberal?
You tie a rope to the anchor before you throw it overboard.

Daily Obama Jokes 07/03/09

How can you tell if a liberal is well hung?
His feet stop twitching.

Thanks to His Obaminess we have so many government officials we have to pack them in like Czardines.

What should liberals do?

While there are many answers we'd all like to give to that question it is one that deserves a little thought. Many of their goals are worthy enough - helping sick people who don't have insurance, for example - the problem is there methods. What they miss is that you can't get a moral end result by immoral methodology. As a result they view government as the resort of first choice and believe in stealing from people for their own aims and beliefs through an immoral and unchecked tax code.
There are other choices.

The Gift Of Giving
The libs think the government needs more money, that taxes aren't high enough. They are entitled to that belief and to act on it Uncle Sam accepts gifts. Each liberal in the U.S. is free to write any size check he wants to the government. If they really felt as they claim this is what they would do.
Let's look at the respected Warren Buffet. He's been for raising taxes of late. He's also stated on national TV. that his secretary pays taxes a higher rate than he does. (remember in previous columns I've talked about how tax increases hit the Henrys, the high earning not rich yet.). I haven't heard of him writing a check to the government voluntarily. In fact when he dies he's leaving something like 38 billion to charity via the

161

Gates Foundation. If government needs money so badly and does such a good job why not leave it to the feds? And if you're so generous why not give it away while you're still alive instead of waiting until you're done playing in the sandbox?

Charity
Liberals are perfectly free to start charitable foundations, tax exempt and deductible yet, to achieve many aims. Want more health care for the uninsured? Start a foundation and open up free clinics across the land. Liberals everywhere could contribute. Fact is if they showed me they were doing a good job I'd contribute, too, As I choose and as I can afford. Instead they try and rip the money out of other people's pocket to have a government that can't wipe its own butt do it.
And that's where we have a problem.

Of course it could well be that these good deeds and such are not the real aim. Perhaps the real aim is power and control over every facet of life in America and of her people. Perhaps most people who call themselves liberal have been duped by a power hungry leadership, with his Obaminess being the worst of the lot, into supporting immoral actions disguised as crusading do gooders.
Could it be, really, just about plain old power after all?

And if you disagree with me, then you, Sir, are worse an Obama promise.

National Ignition Facility. Fusion power for the future.

Daily Obama Jokes 07/04/09

Happy Fourth Of July

Independence Day.
It's a day when once again I must ponder why
keep this country together? We have two
different groups far apart in how they think the
country should be run. No matter which comes to
power the other half feels oppressed.
Ultimately it is senseless and strife filled. There is
no need. Liberals should be allowed to have their
own system Conservatives theirs.
We are two nations divided spiritually and
intellectually to an extreme.
Should we not, therefore, be two nations in fact
as well?
We are on the verge of tyranny .of the minority
by the majority, the anathema of democracy. It
is time to split into two, For two groups to each
go their own way. To become two separate
nations, each living according to the dictates and
principals it loves.
Time for a new Independence Day.

Happy Fourth Of July

Look for all these Politicsisfun.com books

Politically Incorrect Blond, Brunette And Redhead
        Jokes.
Little Willie's Rhymes and Crimes
Autistic Loves: Vignettes Of Joy
2008 T-Shirt Wit And Wisdom
Success Secrets Of The Illuminati
Politically Incorrect Female Chauvinist Jokes
        About Men
Love And Sex Proverbs Around The Globe
Politically Incorrect Sick Jokes
Politically Incorrect Liberal Obama Jokes
Tarot: A Basic Primer

All are exclusively available through Amazon.com

Search on the author's name, James Buffington, for
these and future titles.

3086028

Made in the USA